Looking at SOLIHULL

by
JOY WOODALL
and
MOLLIE VARLEY

Illustrated by K. J. Startin

For Molly

© Joy Woodall 1987
  Mollie Varley
ISBN 0 9504039 5 4
ISBN 0 906869 01 3
Published jointly by Joy Woodall, Solihull and
The Libraries & Arts Department of Solihull Metropolitan Borough Council
Printed by Louis Drapkin, Allcock Street, Birmingham

Illustration overleaf — The Tanyard Cottages, Warwick Road

Contents

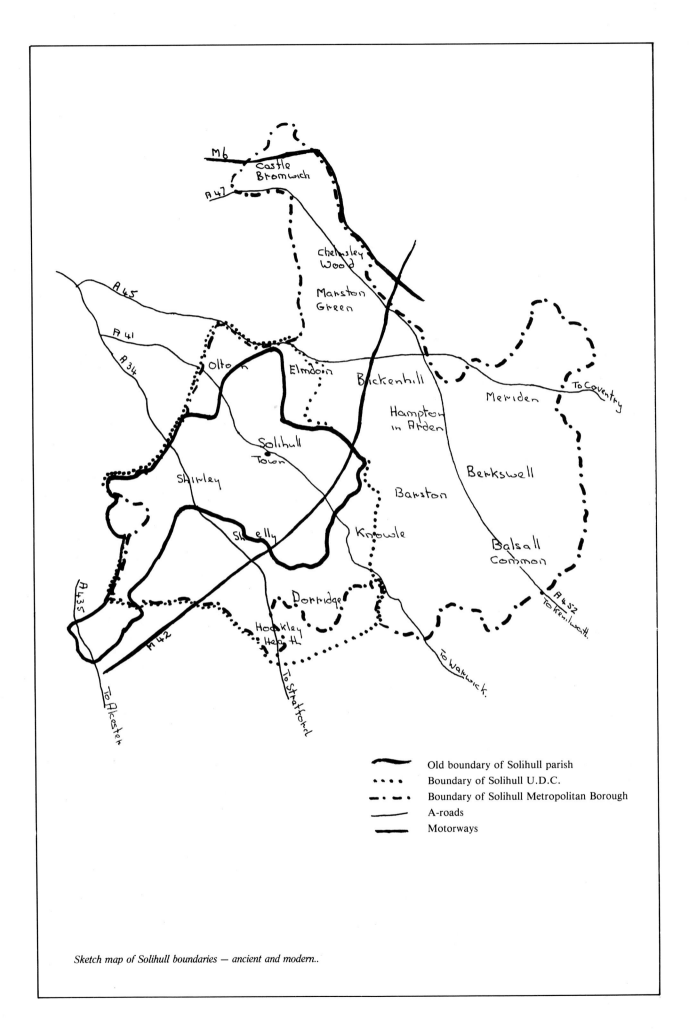

M6

Castle Bromwich

A47

Chelmsley Wood

Manston Green

A45

A41

A34

Olton

Elmdon

Bickenhill

Meriden

To Coventry

Hampton in Arden

Solihull Town

Shirley

Berkswell

Barston

Shelly

Knowle

Balsall Common

A435

M42

Dorridge

Hockley Heath

To Kenilworth

A452

To Warwick

To Alcester

To Stratford

▬▬▬▬	Old boundary of Solihull parish
••••	Boundary of Solihull U.D.C.
▬·▬·▬·	Boundary of Solihull Metropolitan Borough
────	A-roads
▬▬▬	Motorways

Sketch map of Solihull boundaries — ancient and modern..

FOREWORD

Shortly after the manuscript of this book was completed Mollie Varley died in her sleep whilst on holiday. She was a most enthusiastic local historian, an excellent researcher and a kind and thoughtful friend.

Mollie and I first met in 1959 at a Birmingham University Extra-Mural class on local history. We became friends, attending classes and meetings together and researching the history of Solihull, Lapworth and other local parishes.

Mollie enjoyed walking the fields and was particularly good at reading the landscape. A founder member of the Solihull Archaeological Group she was a keen 'digger' and walked and researched Solihull, Tanworth and other parishes with various members of the Group.

Our first publication, *Solihull Places Names*, was followed by *Solihull As It Was* on which we collaborated with Sue Bell, and *Welcome to Solihull*. We always planned to write in more depth on certain aspects of Solihull's history but for various reasons our proposed project was continually delayed. This year, however, we were determined to produce *Looking Back at Solihull*.

As always thanks are due to many people who have assisted us in our work. For their generous gesture of making their own researches available to us I thank Leighton Bishop; Dr. Denis Gray; Stephen Price, and members of the Solihull Archaeological Group. For permission to reproduce their photographs I thank Dr. Denis Gray; Lloyds Bank, Solihull; Local History Department, City Museum and Art Gallery, Birmingham; Solihull Central Library, and Warwick County Record Office. For their professional assistance my thanks are due to the staff at Lichfield Joint Record Office; Dr. R. Bearman and the staff at the Shakespeare Birthplace Record Office; Mrs. Sue Bates of Solihull Library, and Mr. M. Farr and the staff at Warwick County Record Office.

I would particularly like to thank Julian Lendon and his staff at Solihull Library for their continued support, co-operation and encouragement, Sue and David for their special help, and Kit for her charming drawings and attractive cover.

Joy Woodall
October 1987

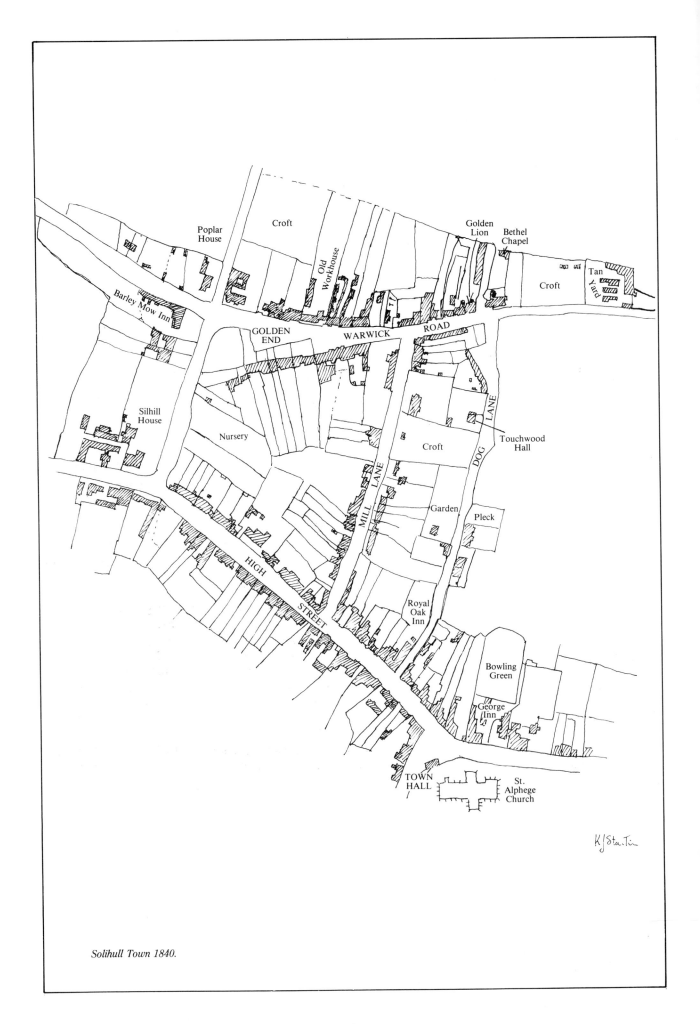

Poplar House

Croft

Old Workhouse

Golden Lion

Bethel Chapel

Barley Mow Inn

Croft

Tan Yard

GOLDEN END

WARWICK ROAD

Silhill House

Nursery

Croft

DOG LANE

Touchwood Hall

MILL LANE

Garden

Pleck

HIGH STREET

Royal Oak Inn

Bowling Green

George Inn

TOWN HALL

St. Alphege Church

K J Stanton

Solihull Town 1840.

A CENTURY OF CHANGE

From Village to Town

Just over a hundred years ago Solihull began to grow, and to change from a quiet semi-rural village into a select and slightly sophisticated small town. The transformation was gradual and began in October 1852 with the opening of Solihull Station (and the Paddington to Birmingham line) by the Great Western Railway Company. In Birmingham, as elsewhere in the country, trade was booming and the workshops of the town of a 'thousand trades' were expanding rapidly. The advent of the train enabled successful business men to work in noisy, smoke-grimed Birmingham but to live and bring up their families in the clean and pleasant atmosphere of Solihull.

There was, however, no great rush of newcomers to Solihull, for there were few 'modern' amenities: until the 1860's no gas or piped water, no pavements or street lights, no newly built villas, and the local tradesmen had little to offer except essential goods. A description of the village written in 1840 was just as valid 20 years later for little if anything had changed —

> 'Solihull consists of four streets, two principal ones — High Street and Warwick Street — and two collateral ones connecting the two others — Mill Lane and Dog Lane [Drury Lane]. It is remarkably neat and rural in its appearance and justly excites the admiration of travellers. Though the houses of the poor are intermingled with those of their richer neighbours, yet no painful disparity offends the eye or impels the beholder to invidious comparisons. An air of comfort and respectibility marks all alike and renders Solihull indisputably a delightful looking town.'

1861 — 'A pleasant village . . .'

The census returns of 1861 reveal that the four streets of the description still made up the village and that they contained a mixture of houses, cottages and shops, although the latter were probably hardly noticeable with their ordinary house-windows and discreet sign-boards. The properties were occupied by the same rich and poor people — labourers, tradesmen, craftsmen, professional men and those of independant means — in all some 220 households, who lived and worked in a closely knit community. There were seven inns, four in High Street — the *George*, the *Royal Oak*, the *Malt Shovel* (now the *Snooty Fox*), the *Mason's Arms* — and three in Warwick Road — the *Barley Mow*, the *Saddler's Arms*, the *Golden Lion*. There were two doctors; three solicitors; a vet, Thomas Proctor; and three policemen. The Police Station and house, occupied by Inspector Joseph Smith, was the only building in New Road. Purpose built in 1851 the Station (now two shops — Gerald and Geoffrey Hassall) had two cells measuring 9ft. by 6ft.6ins., to house prisoners. New Road had been realigned and made in 1829, hence its name. In the road, in a spinney backing onto Malvern Park, was one of the two public water pumps in the village, for those who did not have a well had to collect all their water from these communal supplies.

Round the corner from New Road was The Square, then considered to be part of the High Street. In earlier centuries the market had been held in the open space of The Square but only occasional fairs — on 29th April for cattle and horses, on the Friday following the 9th September for hiring servants, and on 12th October for cheese and cattle — now came to the village. These were red letter days in the local calendar for people from a wide area thronged the streets and there were side shows and roundabouts.

The Square was dominated by the church, charmingly covered with ivy and creeper but under which it was slowly crumbling away. Opposite was the *George*, the best of the village inns. Presided over by Mrs. Elizabeth Stewart, the landlady since 1828, it was the dining and meeting place of the local gentlemen, and of certain clubs.

In High Street and The Square there were several handsome buildings with facades of fine local brick. One of the best was the *Royal Oak*, tall and elegant with a pedimented doorcase. It was kept by Mrs. Hammond who, with her late husband Thomas, had been the host since at least 1830. A number of the houses had wisteria trailing over them which, abundant with flowers in early summer, beautified the street; the finest specimen, was reputedly, that covering the front of the *George*. Outside Lime Tree House (now The Manor House) was a row of nine very tall lime trees which quite overshadowed that part of the street.

There were more tradespeople in High Street than in any other street of the village. As well as the expected butcher, baker and grocer, there was a shirt maker; a stay maker, Letitia Earps; and a tinman, George Wall, who repaired metal utensils, kettles, pots and saucepans. In this street too lived a doctor, William Moall, and the solicitors; Richard Chattock at Northmede Cottage (long demolished, the site now being part of the Link Road car park), George Harding who lived and had his office next door to the *George*, and Sydney Mitchell who occupied a large house with a portico (now the Western Jean Co. and Mackays). The four inns were kept by women all, except Mrs. Whitehouse at the *Mason's Arms*, being elderly widows. John Whitehouse farmed at Libbards Farm whilst his wife looked after the inn.

High Street in 1853. The three storey house, left, is now the Western Jean Co. and Mackays.

Occasionally the drovers with their cattle would pass through the village filling the street and blocking it from end to end. The animals moved slowly, at their own pace and were never hurried as they made their way to Birmingham market.

Of the four streets, Dog Lane (now called Drury Lane and three times its original width) had the fewest houses (22), mostly cottages in rows occupied by labourers, a 'salt-seller' and the 'letter deliverer', presumably the contemporary name for the postman. There was one large house in the lane, Touchwood Hall, newly built in 1712. It was occupied by Mrs. Madeley, a widow, and her two unmarried daughters, and had several outbuildings and a gazebo at a corner of the garden. Mrs. Madeley owned the Tanyard, situated in Warwick Road, which was managed by her son Charles (the offices of the Church of Jesus Christ of the Latter Day Saints now stand on this site). Apart from the few houses Dog Lane was lined with gardens and small fields, and the second public water pump was situated here.

In Mill Lane the 39 houses sheltered a complete cross section of the community; retired people, two working farmers, numerous craftsmen, the Excise Officer, an ostler, several labourers and John Lomas, a portrait painter. James Hastings alias Crump, known to the village as Jimmy, was described in the census as 'labourer' but he was also a water carrier. In a barrel on wheels, drawn by a donkey, he carried water from Streetsbrook Brook and other local springs to village householders who preferred spring water or who had no well and would not use the public pump. A charge of ½d (¼p) per bucket was made.

Touchwood Hall c.1910.

The public water pump outside Smith's cottage, Drury Lane c.1860's.

Jimmy Crump with his water cart in High Street.

Poplar House, Lode Lane c.1905.

Mill Lane was very slightly wider and straighter than Dog Lane but it had less open space. All the houses had gardens however, several of the groups of cottages being surrounded by very large plots, and there was a croft which stretched through from Dog Lane.

Warwick Road (from the present Lode Lane to Hampton Lane) contained 57 houses and cottages. Included were the *Barley Mow Inn* and Curtis House, then the only two properties in what is now Poplar Road, and considered to be part of Warwick Road. The inn, kept by Sarah Perry, an elderly widow, was a low, white building, the interior being below the level of the road. The house next door, named after their family, was occupied by Charles and Dorothy Curtis. Their jovial, fox-hunting father was the rector of Solihull, and of Birmingham, from 1789 until his death in 1829.

Opposite the *Barley Mow* stood Poplar House (now the site of Brueton Gardens and the Coronation Clock), a pretty house with 21 Lombardy poplars in the garden. Across the narrow entrance to Lode Lane, on the corner with Warwick Road, lived Dr. Thomas Lowe. His large, old house, The Limes (now called Quinet House) had been the home of successive doctors since 1761. Past Dr. Lowe's garden were other old houses including a row of three converted from the old Workhouse, built in 1742.

The Golden Lion Inn, Warwick Road.

There were many cottages in Warwick Road; a row of 12 standing at the rear and to the side of the newly erected *Saddler's Arms*, with more close to the *Golden Lion Inn* and in the Tanyard. In some of the latter lived the tanner's labourers, the other cottages being occupied by farm workers, a chimney sweep, railway employees, gardeners and minor tradesmen.

Beyond the Tanyard, towards Hampton Lane, there were two fields and a long narrow pond, then Bradford House (now the Bursar's Office to Solihull School). The opposite side of the road, from Dog Lane to New Road, was also devoid of houses. Surrounding the village, on all sides, were fields, narrow lanes, and here and there a group of cottages or a farmhouse and everywhere an abundance of trees.

Throughout the 1860's and 70's Solihull was said to be 'rather on the increase since the opening of the . . . Railway, affording an agreeable place of residence for the families of Birmingham merchants and others', and indeed this was the case.

1880's '. . . a pretty, quiet country town'

By the mid-1880's a great many changes had taken place, and Solihull could claim to have become a small town. A considerable amount of building had occurred both within and on the edge of the village thus extending it boundaries. About ten houses had been built at the town end of Lode Lane and at least a dozen, many of them semi-detached, in New Road. Two new roads, Homer Road and Herbert Road, had been cut through the fields between the church and the station, in the former there were four houses and in the latter two; all were large with three storeys. The Lode Lane houses were also substantial; there were four detached residences with very big gardens (three still exist — The Grove, Brook House and the house now Ruckleigh School) and almost opposite were seven houses in a continuous row, these too were spacious with sizeable gardens. One of these Lode Lane houses was occupied by Joseph Pippett, a designer, his wife, and family of 16 children, some of whom had uncommon names; Elphege, Oswald, Etheldreda, Raphael, Gregory and Gabriel. Several of them were artistic and grew up to be wood carvers, painters, and sculptors. Most of the houses contained large households, six having 66 occupants, including servants, between them. Large families were quite common amongst the manufacturers and merchants of paper, glass, hardware, hinges, and bedsteads, of metal and of brass, who lived in Lode Lane. (The block of seven houses was demolished in the 1970's to make way for the Hospital extension having served for many years as Netherwood Maternity Unit and the Nurses Home).

The houses in New Road were smaller and less grand; they attracted retired people, successful tradesmen, and widows and spinsters of independent means. (Some of the properties were pulled down to make way for Brueton House, but the majority remain).

Built by 1886 these houses have recently been replaced by offices — St. Catherines Court. Photograph c.1910.

In Warwick Road six large villas, four of them semi-detached, had been built opposite what is now Solihull School. They were erected on the site of a brick-yard, where the bricks for Bradford House had been made earlier in the century. The first of these villas to be erected, Ash Cottage, was built for Miss Caroline Martineau as a Convalescent Home for poor children from West Bromwich, where she lived. Later Mrs. Evans, the wife of the rector, took over the Home and by 1887 it had moved to larger premises in Widney Manor Road (now demolished and replaced by houses — 15 and 15a). Further along Warwick Road on the corner of Drury Lane stood the Congregational Church erected in 1883. It was built on land given by Charles Madeley, the tanner, to accommodate an increasing congregation which had outgrown the old noncomformist chapel, known as the Bethel, in Union Road; the latter became their Sunday School and Church Hall. (The Congregational Church and the Bethel were demolished in the 1960's, the former site is now occupied by Beatties and the latter by the John Palmer Hall).

The Congregational Church, Warwick Road. The small houses, beyond, in Drury Lane were built c.1904.

Broomfield, Warwick Road. Demolished c.1939.

13

▲ *Warwick Road c.1860. The houses above are thought to have stood near the Saddler's Arms.*
▼ *They were replaced by the five villas below, later these had shop extensions built in the front gardens. Demolished 1960's.*

Some of the cottages and houses between Mill Lane and the *Saddler's Arms* had been demolished and replaced by a row of five substantial villas — The Beeches, The Cedars, and Jessamine House. Four of these were occupied by middle class newcomers including Dr. Ernest Hardwicke, a young general practitioner, but the fifth was a boarding house run by Miss Mary Ann Chinn, who was related to the landlord of the *Barley Mow*. Her guests were chiefly professional men and merchants, young Dr. Palmer, probably an assistant to Dr. Hardwicke, and Francis Horton, a wine merchant. Her brother, Frederick, a tax collector and the assistant overseer of the poor, lived with Miss Chinn and their aunt. In the Queen Anne house opposite (now the offices of Roland Evans, solicitor) Mrs. Harriet Guest ran a similar establishment with her sister, mother and son. Her lady lodger was a daily governess, Georgina Ellis, and her two male boarders gas fitters from Lincolnshire.

The Tanyard had closed down in 1867 and the owner, Charles Madeley, retired. His elderly unmarried sister occupied Touchwood Hall, the family home, so he lived in a new house, Broomfield, which he had built on the site of the bark-shed of the tannery. The workshops had been converted into cottages and there were now nine, pleasant and roomy, within the Tanyard area. They were occupied by labourers, gardeners, a laundress, a char-lady, a carter and a brick-maker. The later, Henry Thorne, had previously been a tanner's labourer.

Warwick Road c.1905. On the right the entrance to Mill Lane, and a high class grocers shop.
On the left cottages, a smithy, the vets' surgery and the entry to 'Deebanks Yard'.
The sign is that of the Golden Lion Inn.

Close to the *Golden Lion* four small houses had been formed, either by converting old buildings or creating new ones 'up the yard', behind the existing houses. They were known locally as 'Deebanks Yard' possibly because the Deebank family, who were small builders, lived nearby in the 1870's, and might have been involved in the conversion. This firm prospered, no doubt benefiting from the building boom in the town. By 1881 James Deebank, with his wife and eight children, was living in High Street in a house close to the *Mason's Arms*; he employed 25 men in his business.

The High Street had changed considerably since 1861; gas street lamps had been installed and a most attractive and distinctive pavement laid; it had a central path of brick sets edged with Rowley Rag cobbles. This had improved walking conditions and made the street look neat, even though the road surface remained rough and dirty. On both sides of the street some demolition of cottages and old properties had taken place and there had been some infilling. The old buildings had been replaced by six semi-detached houses (now occupied by Fosters; Timpsons and Paul Rocky; the Health Food Centre and Four Seasons Restaurant), a large butchers shop and house (now the National Westminster Bank), and one or two small houses. Beyond the Catholic Church and the newly made Herbert Road were four new, large houses, three together (now St. Martin's School) and one further on — Arden Lodge (now demolished). Two other impressive houses which stood opposite — Fernleigh and Sutton Lodge (now the site of the Link Road, and Station Road shops) — extended this end of the town towards the station.

High Street was a popular place of residence for the newcomers and for old residents who wished to live at the best address. Many of the existing properties had been 'improved' by adding bay windows, putting in extra storeys, refacing or rendering and by general modernisation. Amongst those living in The Square and High Street were two vets, Alfred Brook Proctor, the son of Thomas Proctor the vet in 1861, and his young partner, Florence J. Insall; their surgery was in Warwick Road. There were two solicitors, Frank Adcock who lived in the 'Gothic House' (now the Pizza Parlour and Imperial Cancer Research Charity Shop) and Sydney Mitchell who had moved to the bottom of the street, probably to a larger house for there were now 13 in his household including five servants. The street was also home to a house agent, William Thompson; a chartered accountant, Edward Russell; an auctioneer, William Endall; an insurance agent and at least eight businessmen including a steel toy maker.

There were still numerous cottages in High Street; the group known as Ramsgate Court (now approximately Bejam and the adjacent footway to the car park) were sideways on to the street and had been considerably extended since 1840 when they were described as 'three tenements'. Some of the cottages may also have been sub-divided, for by 1881 there were 13 families, some of whom had lodgers, living in this comparatively small area. Covered in creeper the cottages were considered to be very picturesque.

The cottages at Ramsgate Court.

High Street c.1870. The site of the timbered cottages is now occupied by Gateway.

High Street from Silhill House c.1890. The building, right, with three small gables is now McDonald's.

17

Drury Lane had also changed since 1861. It had been given a new name and many of its open spaces had been built on. In addition to the Congregational Church there were several pairs of neat semi-detached villas, a row of small houses, and on a piece of land owned by Solihull Charity Estate, a building known as Church House had been erected. However Touchwood Hall and many of the old cottages still survived. Altogether there were 36 houses in the street, the residents being more mixed than previously, for retired people, prosperous tradesmen, and those of independent means were occupying the new houses.

Villas in Drury Lane. Photograph c.1950's.

Mill Lane had changed less than Drury Lane, although it too had more houses than in 1861. The residents were still very much a cross section of the community including farm workers, an architect, brick layers, a schoolmaster, an artist from America and George Wall, the tinman, who had moved from High Street. Many householders had lodgers and there were very few people who lived alone. The large gardens and open spaces which remained made Mill Lane a pleasant and popular place to live.

Many of the new houses in the town had names and several of the old ones acquired them, especially if the occupiers were newcomers, for houses were not yet numbered. Station Road and Poplar Road were named, the latter after a row of poplar trees which once lined the south side of the road; becoming unstable after a storm they had to be felled. The Square became the address of those whose houses faced the church and Park Road began at Park House (now part of the *George*). Dog Lane lost its original name and became Drury Lane, reputedly after a group of strolling players had performed in a barn at Touchwood Hall. For a time in the 1870's Mill Lane had been renamed New Street but by the 1880's had reverted to its old name.

By the mid-1880's in High Street particularly, but elsewhere in the town as well, there were many more shops and a wider choice of goods than in the 1860's and 70's. The majority of the shopkeepers had exchanged the small house-windows for large plate-glass panes through which displays of goods could be easily seen. There were several butchers, bakers and high class grocers: Mrs. Mary Ann Lea, provision merchant, specialized in tea and John Vize was a pastry cook and confectioner. It was also possible to buy gowns and mantles, gloves, hosiery, haberdashery and materials of all kinds, including silks, from James Leal at The Central Drapery and

Buildings of many periods — medieval to Edwardian — in Mill Lane c.1950's.

Looking towards Silhill House c.1905. On the right Lea's, grocers, and next door, The Gables, occupied by Dr. Bernays.

Fancy Bazaar (now Princess Kitchens), poultry and fish from Gilbert and Richards (now Clarks, greengrocers), and musical instruments, including pianos and organs from Frank Fairfield, who could also arrange hire purchase. Bradbury sewing machines were available from James Williams, a tailor who specialized in breeches and riding habits, whilst Western and Wheeler sewing machines might be purchased from Charles H. Stone. The machines were a side-line for Stone was by trade a boot and shoe maker; a second side-line was the agency for Pullars 'dyers to the Queen'. Elsewhere in the street Miss Emily Bragg also undertook dyeing and cleaning for few materials, apart from cotton and linen, could be washed. At this time most garments were made to measure rather than bought off-the-peg. There were numerous dress-makers, tailors and milliners in the town, all competing for trade and all eager to serve the high class customers who shopped in the High Street. Even umbrellas were made to order by Charles Wright who lived in a cottage in Park Road and later moved to the bottom of High Street.

Those wealthy enough to have a bank account were able to deposit money at Lloyds who built their present premises and opened an office (it was not called a branch until 1894) with two staff in 1877. They did not use the whole building but shared it with the Solihull Gas Company and the Solihull Union office. A Penny Savings Bank for people who wished to save in a smaller way was available at the office of Mr. Mitchell, solicitor, opposite the church, from 1880. It was open every Saturday from 10.00 to 11.00 a.m. and from 6.00 to 7.00 p.m. and offered 2½ per cent per annum interest. The Trustees were three leading men of the town, the rector, Canon Charles Evans, Charles Madeley and Mr. H.H. Chattock, magistrate and landowner, who lived and farmed at Silhill House situated on the corner of Poplar Road and Station Road.

Lloyds Bank, Poplar Road in 1880.

Next door to Lloyds Bank was the Public Hall, built by a private company in 1876 to serve a variety of purposes. It was used for the Petty Sessions, for Balls, Assemblies, concerts and meetings of all kinds. Afternoon and evening events were very popular and well attended. According to the *Parish Magazine* they included a course of six weekly lectures to women on health; annual 'bountiful tea parties' for up to 150 'aged matrons', and 'Entertainments consisting of readings and songs rendered by residents of Solihull and the neighbourhood'. The Hall was also used for an annual mid-day dinner for 'labouring men of 60 years and upwards'. All the charitable meals were given with the best of intentions and appear to have been received with grateful thanks.

Previously all such social gatherings and court sittings had been held in the Town Hall, a small late 18th century building which stood on an ancient site in The Square, just within the churchyard wall. The Town Hall fell out of use when the Public Hall was built, and with some regret it was decided to demolish it. Thomas Bragg, another successful local builder, charged £12 for doing the job in 1880.

The horse-drawn Fire Engine which had been kept in a building adjoining the Town Hall, was re-housed in a new Fire Station at the rear of the *Barley Mow*. For some years Solihull had received assistance from the Birmingham Brigade but this was no longer available, consequently Solihull and District Volunteer Fire Brigade was formed. A group of Vice-Presidents supported it financially and almost at once ordered a new machine, made by Messrs. Merryweather, which was purchased through members subscriptions and monetary gifts. The Solihull men who had manned the Engine under Birmingham continued to do so led by their Foreman, T. Thompson who held the Engine key.

KJStanton

The Town Hall in The Square, demolished 1880.

For those who could afford to pay for their pleasure in reading there was a Subscription Library and for those who could not, the Working Men's Reading Room in the High Street supported, in part, by the evening 'Entertainments' at the Public Hall. There were several clubs and societies for men — The Cricket Club, the Caledonian Corks, the Becher Club, and the Oddfellows — the three latter being Friendly Societies for sick benefit. The Bechers and the Oddfellows each had anniversary days starting with a service in the church. The Oddfellows first marched in procession around the town with their beautifully embroidered banner then 'dinner' followed, the Oddfellows at the *George* and the Bechers at the school room. After the annual report and business the members of Bechers and their families enjoyed sports and dancing, usually in the Rectory grounds.

For the women there were good works and charity — the Ladies Charity and the Ladies Working Society or Dorcas Society which made 'useful garments to be sold to the poor at reduced prices in the winter'. The subscription was 5s. (25p.) per year and the wives and daughters of the leading families of the town belonged. There was also a Junior Dorcas run by the young ladies who did similar work.

A group of Solihull women gathered outside the Rectory, perhaps after a Working Society meeting.

Men and women, rich and poor, belonged to the Clothing and Medical Clubs. The better off, who were Honorary Members, paid an annual subscription to each club varying from 5s. to £3. The less well off paid between 1d. (½p.) and 6d. (2½p.) per week to the Clothing Club and 1½d. per week per family or ½d. per single person to the Medical Club; children over 14 years living at home were regarded as single people. At the end of the year the sums were repaid with a bonus to spend on clothing or coal. In time of sickness a ticket, price 1s. (5p.), was obtained from the Rectory and this entitled the purchaser to medical attendance and medicine for six months. Confinement tickets cost 5s. 6d. (27½p.).

Solihull was well served for religious services. Most denominations were catered for, the Roman Catholics at St. Augustine's, the nonconformists at Christ Church and the Church of England at the parish church of St. Alphege, stripped of ivy and thoroughly restored in 1879; all were strongly supported. Church House in Drury Lane was used by the St. Alphege congregation as a church hall, the Sunday School was held there and also the Subscription Library. Dinners for the old and poor were given there and in time of crisis a soup kitchen for the needy opened daily.

From 1870 all children were obliged to go to school, although many parents thought it unnecessary. The majority of the children in the town attended the Elementary School situated next door to the church in Park Road (now St. Alphege C.E. School). Originally the Lower School of the Free Grammar School, it had moved to a new building on this site in 1850. Extensions were made in 1862 to accommodate girls and in 1872 for an infants department. By the mid-1880's it was bursting at the seams, and a new site was being considered for a boys only school in Mill Lane. At this time tuition at the school was not free, a charge of 2d. (1p.) per week per child being made. Other children, not all of them Catholics, attended St. Augustine's School which had opened in 1885 in Herbert Road at the rear of the church. Father Michael O'Sullivan, the much loved priest at this period, was responsible for its foundation. His niece, Miss Mary O'Gorman came from Ireland to be its head teacher and under her watchful eye and strict discipline the children received an excellent if simple education. She remained at the school for many years and is still remembered and much respected by her now elderly pupils.

Having ceased to be a church hall, Church House, Drury Lane, became a house and an office. Photograph c.1950's.

There were also several small private schools in the town. Mrs. Helen Burden's, described as a Ladies Boarding School in 1880 but as a Boys School a few years later, occupied the house in High Street previously occupied by Sydney Mitchell. Higher up the street, at Linden House (now part of the *George*) Elizabeth and Jane Bryett had their Boarding School. With a staff of two teachers and two pupil teachers they taught about ten boarding pupils, plus day girls. The Misses Elizabeth and Martha Edwards ran a Ladies School, at first in New Road where they had boarders, and later in Warwick Road. In Warwick Road too was Mrs. Mary Pitman's school.

For older boys there was the Grammar School, an ancient foundation which for centuries had occupied Malvern House, Park Road. It ceased to be a free school in 1850 and in 1882, with about 45 pupils, moved to new and much larger premises in Warwick Road. The school expanded rapidly and by 1884 there were 80 boys, the fees being £7 10s. 0d. per annum for existing pupils and £9 0s. 0d. for new boys. Various scholarships and exhibitions were offered and these were often won by boys from the Elementary School.

On the fringe of the town stood Malvern Hall, the home of the Greswold family for two centuries. The Greswolde Williams, descendants of the original family, who occupied the house in the 1880's were frequently away from home and took little part in the life of the town. The park, enclosed by a paling fence, was private and rarely opened to the local people except on very special occasions.

Below the church stood the Rectory, a large brick house with south facing rooms overlooking a beautiful garden, at the foot of which was an avenue of trees (now Rectory Gardens, Rectory Road and Ladbrook Road). Here the rector lived in some state, he, his wife and four sons being cared for by a cook, two housemaids, a lady's maid, a nursery maid, a kitchen maid and a coachman. It was Canon Evans who brought to an end the holding of the Fairs in The Square, for on such days hordes of people came to Solihull from Birmingham by train. They brought noise and discord to which he objected and consequently the Fairs were stopped.

At the other end of the social scale was the Workhouse situated in Union Road (now part of the Hospital). Built in 1838 to house the poor of the 12 parishes in the Solihull Union, the Workhouse had 92 inmates in 1881: 55 men, 16 women, and 21 children, including James Hastings, once the water-carrier. They were supervised by Robert and Mary Ann Layton, the Master and the Matron.

Parish to Rural District Council

At this period there was little in the way of local government, nationally or locally, and the changes which took place in the town were effected without the restrictions, delays and frustrations which now hamper any alteration in the environment, even if it is acknowledged to be necessary.

The only form of local administration from about the 18th century until 1872 was the parish, and the Board of Guardians created in 1836 to oversee the welfare of the poor. The Solihull Board of Guardians, responsible for the poor of 12 local parishes — Baddesley Clinton, Barston, Bushwood, Elmdon, Knowle, Lapworth, Nuthurst, Packwood, Tanworth-in-Arden, Temple Balsall, Yardley and Solihull — was made up of clergy, landowners, farmers and professional men. There were 24 members, 20 of them elected, each parish having one representative and the larger parishes up to four. It was the poor of these parishes who might be sent to the Workhouse at Solihull.

Under the Public Health Act of 1872 the Board of Guardians became the Solihull Rural Sanitary Authority and was given increased power with regard to public health, drainage and sewage matters. Twelve members of the Guardians were elected to act as the Sanitary Authority and they met each fortnight. They dealt with matters relating to the poor in the morning session and with public health in the afternoon. Bye-laws were issued regarding the control of common lodging-houses, slaughter houses, the removal of nuisances, also new roads and buildings.

The town did have sewers of a sort but they discharged into the River Blythe, which was unsatisfactory. A site was sought where a purification plant could be built but the demand for land in Solihull parish, generally, was such that prices were too high for the Sanitary Authority to compete. At length a site was leased near the canal at Catherine de Barnes and by the 1880's the town had a satisfactory sewage system.

Solihull was fortunate that it had no slums and that middle class housing predominated, for there were few outbreaks of the dreaded diphtheria. The overall death rate in the town in 1878 was 17 per thousand head of population, against the national average of 22 per thousand in 1871 and 19.4 per thousand in 1885.

In 1894, under the Local Government Act, the Solihull Rural Sanitary Authority was swept away and replaced by Solihull Rural District Council. The new Council had 18 members, most of them of the same social group as served the Guardians and the Sanitary Authority. They were concerned with the affairs of 11 of the same parishes, the exception being Yardley which acquired its own District Council.

From the start of its work the R.D.C. established a quite sophisticated committee system with standing committees on finance, allotments, sanitary and public works, education, general purposes and health. Several officers were appointed; a part-time clerk at a salary of £137 10s. 0d. (£137.50p.) per annum; a shared medical officer, and a surveyor at a salary of £175 per annum. The latter, Mr. A.E. Currall, who was regularly to be seen out and about in his pony and trap, later had two assistants — a treasurer and an inspector of nuisances. Solihull had placed its foot on the first rung of the ladder of Local Government.

'. . . no longer calm and peaceful'

The changes which Old Silhillians saw in the village between the 1860's and the mid-1880's were considerable and to them probably as disturbing as those which occurred in the town a century later. New, more sophisticated people arrived bringing fresh ideas, work, trade and a degree of affluence. The population increased, but not dramatically; the 1861 census figure of 3,329 people living in the whole parish of Solihull (of 11,000 acres), had risen to only 4,510 in 1881; of these about 1,600, some 330 households, lived in the town. In the following decade the figure swelled to 5,053 and many local residents began to feel uneasy about the future. In 1892 a short piece appeared in the *Parish Magazine* expressing the concern which was then abroad —

> '. . . Speculative builders are beginning to look at Solihull and menace its open spaces. Hideous red brick houses are creeping gradually along the Warwick Road like a line of infantry invading the town. Our rusticity is doomed. As the population increases, and the demand for transit to the City grows, buses will doubtless run into the town . . . The tendency of the time is vandalistic and when the . . . current once fairly sets in the direction of Solihull there will be no stopping it . . . The sacred soil of the old Market Square will be ruthlessly upturned and carted away to be replaced, maybe with macadam . . . The gas which superceded the 'farthing dips' will in turn give place to electric light. Who knows but that Solihull will have a market hall of its own and maybe a Library and Public Swimming Baths?'

Despite these views and worries Solihull continued to expand. New houses, most of them good sized villas or five to eight bedroomed detached properties, were erected at the town edge in Warwick Road, Church Hill Road, Blossomfield Road, Homer Road and Herbert Road, all of which were convenient for the station. The despised houses in Warwick Road were very similar to those which now form the core of the St. Johns Hotel and of Eversfield School; there were many more, but they have now been swept away.

Whilst local people lived in dread of further changes those who looked on from the bustling, crowded streets of Birmingham thought Solihull quaint and very old fashioned. At the weekends people from Birmingham 'put in an appearance in great numbers so that Solihull is no longer calm and peaceful'. An article in the *Birmingham Daily Mail* of November 1903 gives a picture of Solihull as seen by its great neighbour at this time —

'. . . a picturesque old world village, which prides itself on being a village . . . Few places within walking distance of a great city have withstood the changing influence of their ever expanding neighbour as Solihull has managed to do up to the present. Stroll up its broad and peaceful High Street and one may imagine that for half a century or more the world has stood still . . . the march of time has brought none of the aggressive modernity so painfully featured upon the environs of the average centre of industrial life . . . Here and there, it is true, the view is altering, and the virgin pastures are giving place to the habitations of man but Solihull has determined to maintain its rural exclusiveness and country quiet. When somebody recently proposed to introduced the telephone a wail of disapproval went up . . . The rushing motor car it accepts only as the grim inevitable. How it came about that Solihull had endured the telegraph or even the railway passeth comprehension. The railway, however, is only tolerated at a distance. Let a stranger seek the whereabouts of the village as he stands outside the station, and his eye will search in vain unless . . . it alights on the tip of the grey church steeple . . . It is a good step to the High Street . . . and the neatly cropped hedges of two lines of villa residences . . . stamp one . . . with an impression of the eminent respectibility of the village. Most of the houses . . . confirm this . . . They wear an air of gentility, of wealth and comfort combined . . . ''Where are the small houses?'' asks the stranger. And the answer comes that there are none — except the cottages. The real explanation is that the landowners do not want them, and will not have them. They mean to keep the place select. So it follows that, save for the needs of those who live and labour in the village, there are no houses built . . . of the common or garden variety. They must cost £500, at the very least, to put up. Only on that condition, 'tis said, can they obtain the necessary land. Needless to say, Solihull does not grow very rapidly.'

During the next few years, in spite of the above comments, Solihull did grow there being just over 10,000 inhabitants by 1911. Many of the open spaces in Drury Lane and New Road were filled, chiefly by the much looked for smaller houses, and rows of similar dwellings were built in the Grove Road area. However, the majority of the properties erected, some singly and others in groups of three or four, were large. Ashleigh Road had been cut by 1904 and there were some houses in The Crescent by 1911.

Throughout the 1920's piecemeal development took place throughout the parish but it was not until the 1930's that more intensive building began and housing estates began to appear. In 1932 the Local Government boundaries were redefined and Solihull became an Urban District Council administering 20,365 acres and a population of 25,373 people.

Ashleigh Road before the first world war.

A servant and a child watch the photographer, c.1917, outside houses between Hermitage Road and Grove Road.

The New Borough

In 1951 Solihull had been an Urban District Council for almost 20 years and the population had risen to very nearly 68,000. The Council petitioned the Privy Council for a Charter of Incorporation as a Municipal Borough and in 1953, following a public inquiry, it was approved. On 24th May 1954 the Borough of Solihull came into existence.

This important occasion in Solihull's history was marked by great celebrations. These actually took place prior to Charter Day for Princess Margaret had consented to visit the town and present the Charter on behalf of the Queen. On the chosen day, 11th March 1954, the Princess travelled to Solihull by train. The morning was bright and sunny as she drove through cheering crowds and flag-bedecked streets to the Odeon Cinema, Stratford Road, Shirley, where the ceremony was to take place. Before a large number of invited guests Princess Margaret presented the Charter Scroll to Councillor R. Douglas Cooper, the Chairman of Solihull U.D.C., who accepted it on behalf of the citizens of the new Borough, now increased to 72,000.

Following the formalities and speeches, the Princess, having a little time in hand, made an unscheduled visit to St. Alphege Church where she made a brief tour of the building. Princess Margaret's next engagement was at the Council House in Poplar Road where she appeared on the balcony to acknowledge the cheers and waves of the multitude of people who filled the road beneath. The newly acquired Civic Regalia and Plate were on display and were inspected by the Princess with great interest — the Mace, a symbol of the royal authority delegated to the Mayor; the Mayor's Chain and Badge of Office and that of the Mayor's consort, together with a fine collection of silver: candelabra, salvers, cups, vases, trays, bowls and other items. All were given to the Borough by private citizens, business firms, other Councils, and local societies and groups to mark Solihull's rise to Borough status. The royal visit was brought to a close by a celebration lunch held at Lyndon School.

Brownies and Guides lining the pavement as Princess Margaret arrives at the Odeon Cinema, Shirley.

On 24th May Solihull officially became a Borough, and Councillor Cooper and his wife the new Mayor and Mayoress. However, this was not the first time that Solihull had had a Mayor, or that it had been a Borough. Indeed, the town was founded in the 12th century as a Borough, and throughout the medieval period and into the 17th century was referred to in documents as 'The Boro', a Mayor being elected annually until at least 1650.

The Armorial Bearings of Solihull

Solihull became eligible to bear its own coat of arms in 1932 when it achieved U.D.C. status. It was 1946, however, before the Council applied to the College of Arms for a grant of armorial bearings. A design was finally approved in July 1948 and the Letters Patent were issued in September of that year.

The Solihull arms were the first to be granted to an U.D.C. in Warwickshire and they remained the same until 1974 when Solihull became a Metropolitan Borough. They were then re-designed to take account of the 11 parishes which henceforward were to be included within the boundaries of Solihull. The new arms were authorised in 1975.

The coat of arms of a town or city usually contain elements which represent its history, industry or environment. There are five parts — the crest, the helmet, the mantling, the shield and the motto — originally each section enabled medieval knights to recognise one another in battle or at tournaments.

The Coat of Arms 1948 to 1974

The Solihull crest is intended to be descriptive of the district. The wreath of silver and red, has the battlements of a tower rising from it; on top of this is an oak tree bearing acorns, and in front of the tree, two sickles with their shafts crossed and blades turned outwards. The tree indicates that Solihull is still rural despite considerable residential development.

The helmet shows the rank of the owner of the arms. The Solihull helmet, of steel, faces sideways with the vizor closed and is the emblem of an untitled person. The ornate drapery hanging from the crest is the mantling. Of silver and red in the Solihull arms it represents the cloth which protected the crusader knight from the sun and is now purely decorative.

The shield bears symbols from the arms of four families who were associated with the Solihull area in the past. In the lower part of the shield is the red Saxon crown referring to Cristina, a princess of the Saxon royal family (the sister of Edgar Atheling and Queen Margaret of Scotland), who held the manor of Ulverlei in 1086, at the time of the Domesday Survey. In the Domesday Book there is no entry under the name of Solihull, for it did not then exist; only *Ulverlei* and *Langedone* (Longdon) are described. By 1087 Cristina had retired to a nunnery, giving her lands, including Ulverlei, to the de Limesi family who, around the middle of the 12th century, planted the market town of Solihull on its present site. As Solihull prospered and grew, Ulverlei and Longdon declined; by 1200 Ulverlei was known as the old town or Olton, and Longdon became little more than a place-name.

When John de Limesi died in 1198 Ulverlei and the new settlement of Solihull passed to his sister, Basilia. In 1213 she married Hugh d'Oddingsell who did much, as did his son and grandson, to encourage trade in Solihull and make it a successful town. The two red pierced stars which are depicted in the upper part of the arms are taken from the bearings of the d'Oddingsell family. The Solihull shield is divided into three parts by two red horizontal bars, these are taken from the arms of the Throckmorton family of Coughton Court, near Alcester. Sir George Throckmorton purchased the manor of Solihull in 1528 and it was held by his family until 1604.

The black running greyhound at the centre of the shield is taken from the arms of the Greswold family who have been associated with Solihull for several centuries. For a short period in the 16th century a Greswold was the lord of the manor of Longdon. A century later, in 1660, Henry Greswold, the rector of Solihull, acquired the Malvern Hall estate; his son, Humphrey, later building the core of the present Hall.

The Solihull motto 'Urbs in Rure' means 'Town in the Country' and continues the rural theme of the crest.

The Arms of the Metropolitan Borough 1974 —

The arms, re-designed in 1975, have two major changes in the shield; an altered helmet; a slightly more flamboyant mantle and motto ribbon, and more subdued colouring. The crest remains the same; the wreath and the mantle are black and silver, and the helmet, still of steel with closed vizor, has changed position to face almost forward.

The shield still bears two red bars, symbols of the Throckmorton family, and the greyhound of the Greswold family, but the Saxon crown and the two pierced stars have gone and been replaced by emblems taken for the arms of the Digby and Aylesford families.

A silver fleur-de-lys on a pale blue background, from the Digby arms, is placed in the lower part of the shield. It represents Chelmsley Wood, Kingshurst and Fordbridge, which once formed part of Coleshill. Simon Digby was granted Coleshill manor in 1496 for his services to the crown and it has remained in the family to the present day. From the 16th century the Digbys were also the lords of Marston Culy, now part of Marston Green.

A black griffin with one paw raised is taken from the arms of the Finch family, Earls of Aylesford. The family has been associated with Bickenhill since the 17th century and held the lordships of the manors of Bickenhill and Meriden since the 18th century.

The motto remains the same, emphasizing the importance of the countryside to Solihull and its people.

◀ *The coat of arms granted to Solihull in 1948 and used until 1974.*

The coat of arms of the Metropolitan Borough of Solihull, ▶ *re-designed in 1975.*

THE OLD BOROUGH

A Medieval Trading Centre

The market town of Solihull, founded as a planted Borough in the 12th century by the de Limesi family, the lords of the manor of Ulverlei, was initially a success. Trade in the town was brisk enough by 1242, for William d'Oddingsell, the then lord of the manor, to acquire a Royal Charter for a weekly Wednesday market and a three-day Fair on the 'Vigil, the Feast and the Morrow of St. Alphege', the 18th - 20th April.

A medieval hall house which stood in Mill Lane until it was demolished in the 1960's. Above — how it may have looked originally.

The town was laid out in a rectangular arrangement of streets, some of which have disappeared. Their names are revealed in medieval deeds: High Street; le Smythestret (now lost); Dogelone; Pottereslone (now lost); le horsetrid (Horse Street = Warwick Road); Warwick Lane; Frydaylane (closed 1819); Myln Lane; and Clariswallone (Glazewell Lane, closed 1819); the last mentioned probably forming the eastern boundary of the town. The streets were lined with houses and shops, each property being erected on an oblong plot of land known as a burgage plot, the narrow end abutting the street.

The town was a Borough, its inhabitants burgesses, free men who paid a money rent for their burgage plot and owed no servile duties or services to the lord of the manor. They were obliged only to obey the rules of good behaviour and fair trading, regular checks being made to ensure that standards were maintained. Those who broke the rules by 'causing an affray', by selling inferior goods, or by giving short weight appeared in the manor court before the lord or his steward and a jury of fellow townsmen, for such transgressions got the town a bad name and drove customers away. Elizabeth Praty, Alice Hawe and Elizabeth Parre were candlemakers who appeared in court accused of making excessive profits, as were Henry Waren and Thomas Cordes, both innkeepers. Fish was an essential part of the pre-Reformation diet, in Lent especially, and William Cokkes and Thomas Walker were both accused of selling fish at too high a price at this time. At the same court, five women who were brewers appeared charged with producing inferior ale, and 11 other women who were ale-sellers also appeared, probably accused of giving short measure. Tempers frequently became frayed; when Henry Prety and Humphrey Swanne disagreed, Humphrey hit Henry and 'drew blood'; consequently Swanne appeared in court and was fined.

Those people who lived outside the town in the 'Forens' as it was called, were not burgesses, and their cases of misdemeanor and nuisance were heard in a separate manor court.

There were many different crafts and trades within medieval Solihull. Street names indicated the presence of smiths, potters, horse dealers, and a miller; other records refer to bakers, sawyers, barbers, joiners, carpenters, chapmen, masons, brewers, chandlers, coopers, hostellers and butchers. In addition there were three trades of some importance in the Borough — cloth making, and leather and metal working. Involved in the cloth trade were weavers; fullers who cleaned the newly woven material of natural oils and grease; sheermen who dressed and prepared the cloth; dyers who coloured it, and tailors who made it up into garments. During the cloth making process the material was stretched out to dry on tenters; frames of wood to which the cloth was attached by tenter hooks. The tenters were place on an open area of land at the north end of Dog Lane known as Teyntours Grene (Tainters Green) which stretched along both sides of Warwick Road, the Green taking its name from the frames.

Solihull High Street as it may have looked in the late medieval period.

Engaged in the leather trade were skinners, tanners, cordwainers and shoers. The metal workers were occupied not only with smithing and making domestic and agricultural ironwork, but also as nailers and 'wyrdrawers' (wire drawers). The latter, initially, made wire by hammering and filing metal slips into rounded threads. At a later period, wire was made by drawing soft metal rods through a hole of smaller diameter; the process was repeated, passing the wire through smaller and smaller holes until the required thickness was achieved. The finished wire was used for making various items including needles, pins, fish hooks and the teeth of carding combs (still used in craft spinning) with which raw wool was teased before spinning.

Throughout the 13th and 14th centuries Solihull appears to have been a profitable market town, but in the long term it failed to fulfil its founders' aspirations. By the early 14th century the Solihull branch of the d'Oddingsell family had died out and from this time the manor no longer had a resident lord, or anyone who actively encouraged and promoted the growth of trade within the Borough. The Wednesday market, the three-day Fair (changed in 1320 to 31st July - 2nd August), and general trading continued but Solihull did not thrive and expand into an important town as did its neighbour and rival — Birmingham.

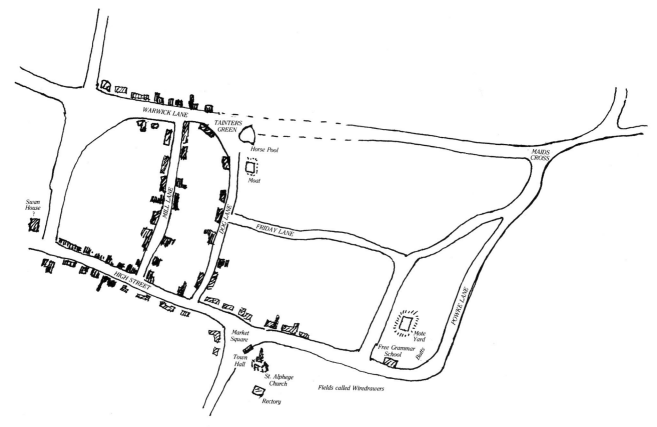

Conjectural map of Solihull in 17th century.

17th Century — In decline

According to a survey of Solihull taken in 1606 the weekly Wednesday market was still being held, as was the three-day Fair. By 1629 however, when a further survey was made, the Fair was held only for one day — Lammas Day — 1st August, and the weekly market was in decline being described as 'in use in some sort'. Only three years later, in 1632, when a third survey was taken, it was stated that 'there ought to be a market kept . . . but the same is now little frequented'. Thus Solihull ceased to be a trading centre although it remained a country town to which people from the surrounding area came from time to time and to which those who lived within the extensive parish of Solihull were obliged to come to church.

In 1629 there were some 45 houses and cottages within the Borough. Almost all had 'a backside' — an area used as a yard or garden — situated at the rear of the burgage plot behind the house-cum-shop-cum-workshop of the occupant. There were still many tradesmen and craftsmen, although not all of them were able to support themselves wholly by their trade. From 1605 'four decayed tradesmen' of Solihull received, annually, a charitable dole of 10s. (50p.) each, the legacy of Mr. Thomas Wheatley of Coventry; 'decayed' did not necessarily mean old in years and with the dole a recipient might be helped through a difficult period. From 1655 the area of residence within the parish and the trade of those receiving the gift is given, and it is possible to determine not only which trades existed in the town but to gain some indication of their success or failure. The dole lists refer to a baker, butchers, carpenters, a carrier, a chandler, cobblers, a cooper, cutlers, a dyer, an edge-tool maker, a flax-dresser, a gardener, glaziers, glovers, hemp-dressers, joiners, labourers, masons, millers, nailers, a pedlar, a point-maker, a ploughwright, sawyers, shoemakers, smiths, tanners, tailors, a tiler, turners, whirlers, weavers, wheelwrights, and a woodcutter. The trades with largest number of dole recipients were those involved with cloth and metal, followed by the workers with wood; only the maltmakers, brewers, beersellers and innkeepers appear never to have fallen on hard times.

Many people in the town had more than one occupation; something to fall back on when their chief craft was not providing an adequate living. Inventories of the period, made for the purposes of probate, show that some tradesmen had agricultural interests. Timothy Swatt, a worker in wood, possibly a carpenter, who died in 1605 had a cow, a heifer and a mare. He was the tenant of 'Pinings house and sertane grounde to the same' which he rented from the Charity Estate for 40s. (£2) per annum. Robert Essex, (died 1606) a comparatively poor man whose trade is not known, had a cow and three pigs, whilst Charles Benton, said in his will to be a shoemaker living in Mill Lane, had a considerable number of animals. He had 14 cattle, nine sheep, five horses, 13 pigs plus 7½ acres of growing crops. In his barn he had one and a half bays of hay, and half a bay elsewhere. His property in Mill Lane consisted of 'a house, barn and backside', his farm land presumably being outside the Borough, in the foreign.

Those who kept a cow in this way made butter and cheese out of the milk. Many houses had a dairy amongst the service rooms, cheese-making utensils, a cheese room in the house, and cheeses stored. William Marston (died 1623) a millwright by trade had 46 cheeses valued at 30s. (£1.50p.) in one of his upper rooms when he died.

Tradesmen who did not supplement their income from agriculture had other side-lines. Many men had brewing equipment, furnaces and vats, and a brew-house or 'yeeling'* house where the brewing took place.

A conjectural drawing of 'The Manor House',
High Street, in the 17th century.

See Glossary p. 65

Robert Higginson, gentleman, (died 1614) by his will left his four coolers in the yeeling-house, valued at £4. and his furnace to his son; they were amongst his most valuable possessions. Others, indeed almost every household, possessed hemp or flax or slippings of yarn; 'hemp growing in the garden', 'hemp unthrashed', 'hemp in the roof', 'knitchings of flax'. Both crops could be dressed, spun into yarn, and woven: flax into linen, and hemp into a coarser cloth; the latter also made strong ropes. Some of the hemp and flax recorded in the inventories was intended for home use after weaving, for almost every house had large quantities of linen: numerous pairs of flaxen and hempen sheets, pillowcases, tablecloths, napkins and towels. Any surplus would have brought in useful extra income. Even the schoolmaster took the opportunity to supplement his meagre salary with hemp; he had a small croft behind the school where he may have grown a little, and in the house, at his death, he had 20 pounds of dressed hemp valued at 13s.4d. (66½p.) and three spinning wheels on which his wife may have spun it into yarn.

Those who could not, or would not, have a second string to their bow lived in poor circumstances and left little to their family at their death. Thomas Cheshire, a labourer, and his wife Anne, had the barest of furniture in their home — a table, a form for seating, a chaff-filled mattress, a cupboard, six pewter plates and a salt cellar; two small kettles, a frying pan, and a pot-hook to hang them on over the fire; a candlestick and a couple of tubs completed the furnishings. The total value of the estate was £6.3s.0d. (£6.15p.) of which £5 was 'invested' in a bond. Edward Holt, 'metalman' was also described as 'gentleman'. Almost everything in his house when he died in 1664 was said to be 'ould', including his clothes, although he himself was probably not aged, having married for the second time in 1654. He had many more worldly goods than the Cheshires, particularly more cooking utensils, but the total value of everything in the house, including a flitch of bacon, his 'budgett' (bag) of tools valued at 6s.8d. (33½p.) and 'a rucke' (heap) of coal, 15s. (75p.) was only £9.2s.4d. (£9.11½p.). He left his tools to his apprentice, Simon Matthews, his best brass candlestick to his grandson, Cyprion Holt, one pound and several items including a pillowcase to his grand-daughter, Joan Steward on her marriage, plus other small legacies. Not forgetting his background as a gentleman, he offered hospitality to his friends at his funeral in the form of cakes, bread, cheese and beer to the value of £5 and left 6s.8d. (33½p.) to the bell ringers. There was nothing in either of these houses to indicate that their owners had alternative skills which would provide extra income in bad times.

Adaptability and versatility appear to have been the way to survival and success in 17th century Solihull. William Marston had money invested in leases and lent out by bonds, which although involving risk, could produce a profit. Charles Benton, the shoemaker, appears to have abandoned his trade for farming, cheese-making, brewing and baking. In his inventory he is described as a victualler (a tavern or eating-house keeper) and he is known to have been a baker and taken lodgers. He gave much time to civic matters and seems to have been one of Solihull's more successful inhabitants.

The Borough was very much a self-regulating unit; there was a petty manor court every three weeks, and a more important manor court, a Court Leet, three times a year at 'Hillarietyde' (January), at Easter, and at Michaelmas (October). At the latter court a Mayor and a Bailiff were elected to serve for a year.

The Bailiff, usually a gentleman or better-off inhabitant, represented both the manor and the parish, for he had manorial duties such as attending all the courts on behalf of the lord of the manor and collecting the fines, as well as being collector of the parish rents. Through charitable bequests made over the centuries, the parish owned a considerable amount of land which was administered by Feoffees (trustees). The Bailiff ensured that the rents were paid, the monies disbursed correctly and the accounts kept. The fines which were collected at the Hilary Leet were given to the Mayor, who paid for the Court dinner with the proceeds.

The petty offences committed were very similar to those recorded previously, all who offended were fined and some were the leading men of the town. John Rice, the constable in 1631, was fined for breaking the law as an ale-seller, and Charles Benton, the Bailiff in 1632 and the Mayor in 1634, was fined both as an ale-seller and a baker and also for not removing his dung-pit from the street. Keeping the town clean and tidy was difficult, people did not clear their ditches, 'Henry and William Benton shall scour their ditches all along Powke Lane' or be fined 5s. (25p.); they threw rubbish into the street, 'no inhabitants . . . shall throw any kind of wood, water or manure on the highway', fine 6s.8d.(33½p.); 'ev'y one shall remove and carry away his mucke out of Dogge Lane', fine 10s.(50p.); they cut wood out of the hedges weakening them and permitted their animals to stray, 'Robert Ladbroke, clerk, allowed his pigs to stray'. This was the rector, who was fined 4d. (1½p.).

Under an Act of 1477 every man was supposed to practise regularly at the Butts. In 1632 Solihull residents were reminded that 'it is ordained that each inhabitant shall have bows and arrows according to the law'. Unfortunately 'the Butts in this borough are ruinous and not in sufficient repair and there is no net at the side there, called in English the Crownett', and the town was fined 3s.4d.(16½p.). The Butts were situated behind the Free Grammar School between Powke Lane alias Butte Lane (previously Glazewell Lane) and the forerunner of New Road, close to an ancient moat called the 'Mote yard', which was possibly the site of the manor house of the early lords of the manor.

There is no mention in the 17th century records of Potters Lane or of Smith Street, these names, and perhaps the lanes themselves, having apparently fallen out of use. The majority of the inhabitants lived in Mill Lane, Dog Lane, Warwick Lane, and High Street, including the Square.

A hearth with cooking utensils.

The houses were timber framed and varied in size and facilities. All had a hall, which was the main living room of the house where the household took their meals, relaxed as best they could on the hard wooden seats, with only a cushion (if they were lucky) to soften them. It was in the hall too that the cooking was done, iron pot-hooks and pot-hangles being fixed in the wide chimney opening, a fire of wood, placed on the floor of the hearth, providing the heat. As the century progressed coal became available but not all households used it. Many houses did have a kitchen but, in Solihull, it was used for the storage of utensils, and perhaps the preparation of food, only. The parlour, a room which the majority of Solihull houses possessed, was the main bedroom containing the best furniture and the most comfortable and valuable bed. The room also doubled as a sitting-room where private business could be conducted and close friends entertained. The rooms upstairs were furnished less well and often contained a strange variety of items being stored — wool, cheese, hemp, corn, apples — even those which were occupied. Some houses had a range of service rooms in addition to the kitchen, these might include a dairy, brew-house, mill-house, boulting-house or yeeling-house.

A cast iron fireback.

A house which did not quite fit into the above pattern was the inn kept by James Russhen (died 1667). The hall was used for dining, the parlour for sitting for there were forms and chairs, half a dozen cushions, and a coal fire in the hearth. Both were probably public rooms for close by was the pantry where large quantities of pewter — dishes, flagons, spoons, chamber pots — were stored with numerous brass and iron cooking pots, pans, and two great barrels. The meals were prepared and cooked in the kitchen over a coal fire.

Upstairs were six rooms; five bedrooms and a cheese room containing 2½cwt. of cheese. The best room was the parlour chamber furnished with two beds, each having a feather mattress, curtains and valences, one set of bed hangings being green and the other yellow. There were tables, chairs, cushions, a cupboard, upholstered stools, a looking glass and pictures on the wall; the last three items were not yet common in the homes of ordinary people and suggest that Russhen was a man of taste and refinement. A coal fire warmed this very comfortable room, probably used only by the landlord's family. The other rooms all had beds with flock mattresses (inferior to feather), although the pillows were of feather. There was other furniture — tables, seating, and a cupboard — in some rooms, but not all. One room was called the Bell Chamber and suggests that the inn was called *The Bell,* the name that the *George Hotel* was known by in 1693 and until 1715.

A bed with curtains and valences similar to that in the parlour chamber at the Russhen's.

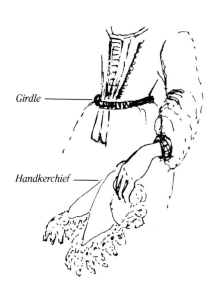

Girdle

Handkerchief

James Russhen brewed the beer he served, having ground the malt in his mill-house. In the buttery there were stored 12 hogsheads and barrels 'with beer in the same', a hogshead holding 52½ imperial gallons. Russhen also had a dairy for he kept three cows; producing, no doubt, milk, butter and cheese for his guests. There were three fat hogs, probably fed on kitchen waste, malt and brew-house refuse and beer dregs, to provide bacon, ham and pork for the inn.

When he died Russhen left to his friends, Thomas Doley and John Taylor, a pair of gloves each as a mourning gift. Such items were purchased from chapmen who sold haberdashery of all kinds. George Banister, probably an itinerant chapman or pedlar, may have been visiting his family when he died in Solihull in 1636, for he had no other possessions except his stock, valued at £62.2s.2d. (£62.11p.). This consisted of pins; handkerchiefs, five being of black lace, valued together at 17s. (85p.); 157 pairs of gloves at different prices from 1½d. to 5s.6d. (½p.-27½p.) per pair; nine muffs at 1s.8d. or 4s. (8½p./20p.) each; purses at 7½d. or 1s.2d. (3p./6p.) each; girdles (belts) and garters, some being of silk. He had 12 fans priced between 6d. and 1s.6d. (2½p.-7½p.) each, and seven screen fans, to protect the face from the fire, at 8d. or 4s. (3½p./20p.) each. There were parcels of ribboning at 2d. to 1s.4d. (1p.-6½p.) per yard; parcels of cambric and holland (fine linen) at 2s.4d. (11½p.) per ell; and scotch cloth (similar to lawn) at 1s. (5p.) per yard. Banister also had eight masks at 6d.(2½p.) each, these were worn by ladies when riding or in inclement weather to save the complexion; bracelets,

Fan

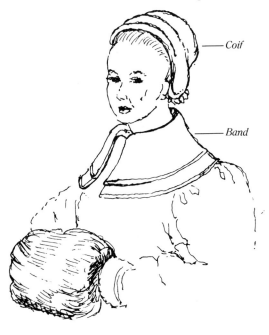

Coif

Band

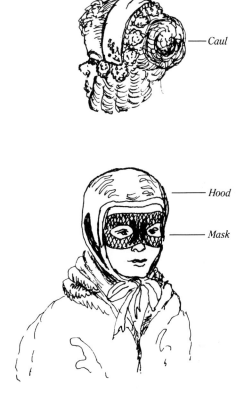

Caul

Hood

Mask

rings and other 'toies' (trinkets); points and laces of silk; hoods 'curled or of taffity' at 2s.4d. (11½p.) each; thread; cauls (netted caps) at 5d. (2p.) each; and 'loome-work' (material made on a loom), 'stoole work' (made on a frame) and 'fferrott' (tape). He had pairs of sleeves at 6d. (2½p.) per pair; framework bands and band strings (collars); 642 yards of bone lace priced between 2½d. and 8s. (1p.-40p.) per yard; and coifs (tight fitting caps) of many sorts — silk, cutwork, drawn thread, and 'for children' — at prices from 1s.2d. to 2s.8d. (6p.-13½p.) each; three of the silk coifs had cross-cloths (forehead bands) and cost 8 groats (2s.9d. = 13½p.) each. The people of Solihull and the surrounding area, ladies, children and men too, clearly kept in step with fashion for many of these items were the mode, and were purchased to refurbish and update existing clothes or to decorate and compliment the new.

HILLFIELD HALL, ITS BUILDER AND OCCUPANTS

Hillfield Hall stands beside a once quiet lane joining Church Hill Road to Libbards Way. To-day the main house is a popular restaurant and its stable block has been converted into an even more popular Bar. New houses and roads are rapidly surrounding the Hall, and its delightful setting of fields and trees will shortly be gone for ever.

Hillfield Hall early this century.

A house and farm were probably first established at Hillfield in the late 13th or early 14th century, a time when severalty farms, known as assarts, were being carved out of the waste or uncultivated land of Solihull. Such farms, created with considerable physical effort, were usually surrounded by a clearly defined ditch and bank boundary. The homestead was often moated for protection and as a symbol of independent status, the moat also doubling as a fish pond.

The Hawes Family of Hillfield

One of the most prominent names in Solihull during the medieval period was that of Hawes. There were several branches of the family who between them owned a considerable amount of land and property in the area. According to the Hawes family papers, one of their number, Thomas Hawes of Shirley, a man 'skilled in the law' bought an estate, including the site where Hillfield Hall now stands, in 1311. What the estate consisted of at that date is not known, but it was probably a farm worked from a moated homestead.

38

The property at Hillfield was owned over the next 250 years by six generations of Hawes, each eldest son being named Thomas, but none of them chose to live there. The first member of the family known to have been resident was William, who is recorded in the Herald's Visitation of 1563 as 'of Hillfield in Solihull'. William Hawes, born in 1531, was the son of Thomas Hawes of Idlicote. In 1562 he married Ursula, the daughter of William Coles, and they settled at Hillfield. By the 1570's William and Ursula had several children and the old moated house was probably both uncomfortable and cramped. They decided, therefore, to build a more convenient house on a site to the south of the moat.

The new house, facing north west, was of red brick with diaper patterns in blue brick and built after the style of a medieval gatehouse. It was three storeys high and had stone mullioned windows. The front had two semi-octagonal turrets with embattled parapets, giving the gatehouse appearance. The north turret contained the main entrance which was through a four-centred stone doorway with an inscription above it in Latin. The west turret contained a spiral staircase winding about a central post from the ground to the top floor. This house, differing totally from anything being built locally at the time, was very much a status symbol declaring the wealth and success of the Hawes family, for contemporary local families, of equal social rank, were living in timber framed houses such as Dovehouse Farm and Old Berry Hall. Brick, although used in some measure, was not generally employed for entire buildings and did not become a common building material, in this part of the country, for another century. The Hawes finishing touch to Hillfield Hall was the tablet over the front door — $_W{}^H{}_V$ 1576 'Hic Hospites in Coelo Cives' — 'Here we are guests, in heaven citizens'. The initials are those of William and Ursula Hawes with the date the house was completed. A typical Elizabethan gesture!

Edmund Hawes, the son of William and Ursula, married Jane Porter some time before 1600 but they did not set up a separate home. The whole family lived together at Hillfield until 1606 by which time Edmund had four children, one having died, and the house must have been overfull. By 1607 Edmund had removed to Shelly, almost certainly to Shelly Farm, and he and his family remained there until after his father's death in 1611.

William Hawes was 80 years of age when he died. From his will it appears that of his eight children four were still living — Edmund, Constance who was unmarried, Ursula who was married to Raphaell Hunte and Elizabeth who was married to William Sheldon.

From the inventory of William Hawes' property, made for the purpose of probate, and taken by four local gentlemen on 11th November 1611, 11 days after his funeral, it is possible to learn something of the interior of Hillfield Hall at this time. William refers to the house in his will as 'my mansion howse' and it was certainly an imposing looking building, but it was only one room deep, although there must have been wings at the rear, probably arranged around a courtyard, because of the many service rooms of various kinds. In the main body of the house there were three reception rooms, the hall, the parlour, and the little parlour which was also a bedroom, plus seven other sleeping chambers including those of the servants. On the top floor there was a long gallery.

The front door opened into the base of the turret which led into the hall, a large room furnished for dining with a long table, six stools and two forms. The seats were not upholstered so there were six cushions to make them more comfortable; there were no chairs. Around the room were two square tables, two cupboards — one having a lock and key, and on one of the tables a desk; this was a box, made of wood, with a sloping lid for convenience when writing. There were two brass candlesticks to provide the light in the room and in the hearth a pair of andirons which were used to support the burning logs.

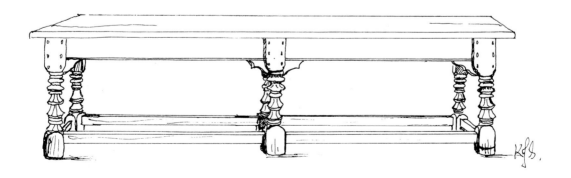

A framed table, and overleaf other furniture, of the type to be found in houses such as Hillfield Hall at this period.

Joined stool

Desk

The parlour was a comfortable room, well furnished and clearly that of a cultured Elizabethan gentleman. It too had a long table with six stools but there were also two chairs. There were 11 cushions to soften the seats, these were of needlework, perhaps embroidered by the ladies of the family. On the walls were two maps, 'certain' pictures, and a clock probably of brass and weight driven. It would have been hung high on the wall, or on a bracket, with its chains and weights hanging below. Around the room were two cupboards, a chess board, and a pair of virginals — an early form of spinet popular with ladies — in a frame. The cupboards were covered with cloths, one being of tent work or petit point. There were three carpets, but these were probably hung on the walls or draped over the table rather than on the floor. One was coloured blue and another was of a material called 'darney'; this was

Court cupboard

Standing bed

a heavy coarse linen fabric originally made at the Flemish town of Doornick, and was used for hangings, carpets and sometimes for servants' clothes. There were two screens to protect the occupants of the room from draughts and in the hearth a pair of andirons, a shovel and a pair of tongs.

The little parlour was a bedroom-cum-sitting-room furnished with a bed, round table, cupboard and stools; a parlour used for both sleeping and sitting was to be found in many houses of all social levels from the 1570's onwards, it being recorded in the homes of the wealthier people first. The little parlour at Hillfield had a great standing bed with a tester, hanging curtains and a feather mattress; carpets covered the table and cupboard and there was a panelled chair. Three of the six stools were upholstered and at the windows there were more curtains hung on rods. Window curtains were quite rare in less affluent homes at this period, most people having shutters or nothing at all.

Upholstered stool

Chair

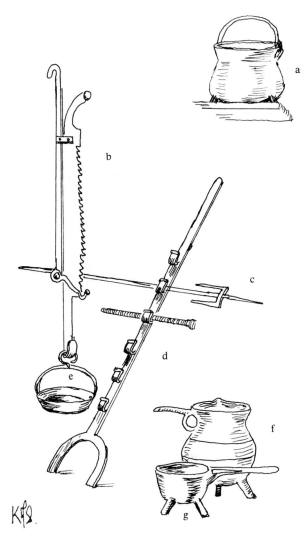

Cooking utensils

a - Cauldron	c - 'Broache'	e - Frying pan	g - Skillet
b - Pot Hangle	d - 'Cobbard'	f - Posnet	

The best bedroom of the house was 'the chamber over the parler' where it is presumed William and Ursula slept. The standing bed had two mattresses, the top one being of feather, two bolsters, three blankets, a pair of pillows of feather plus a pair filled with down — the ultimate in warmth and comfort. There were six curtains round the bed, hung on five rods, and a coverlet of Arras. This was a rich tapestry fabric on which figures and scenes were woven in colour. A map decorated the wall and there was a chair, and two stools upholstered in needlework. The cupboard had a green cloth on it and there were two large cushions covered in silk. This comfortable and colourful room must have been quite cosy on winter nights with a bright log fire burning in the hearth.

The other sleeping rooms were all well furnished even 'the serving mens chamber' having beds with feather mattresses, rather than the flock or chaff filled ones usually given to servants. The rooms over the hall and little parlour both had curtains to the windows, the latter also containing two cross-bows and some armour.

On the top floor was the gallery which ran the whole length of the house. Decorated with maps and pictures it was used for exercise during inclement weather and was a fashionable feature of an Elizabethan house. Little Moreton Hall, in Cheshire, a small country house of contemporary date and also owned by a successful middle class family has a similar long gallery. Within the gallery was a 'closet', described by William Hawes in his will as his 'studie'. Here he sat on a stool at his gilded desk which was placed on a little table. The room also contained 'six drawinge boxes', a coffer containing 'certeine implementes', 'a gilded box', a [magnifying] glass and some books.

On the ground floor was the kitchen, well equipped with utensils, where the food was cooked over an open wood fire situated at ground level on the hearth of a large, wide chimney. In the chimney was fixed an iron bar on which seven pairs of pothooks and hangers were suspended. From these were hung a variety of pots and pans of brass and iron as well as 10 kettles, for heating the water. There were andirons and cobbards (cob irons), five spits, three dripping pans, two skimmers, two cleavers, two iron peels, and a pair of bellows, a pestle and mortar, a gridiron, two frying pans, a 'great salte chest' and six candlesticks for lighting.

Adjoining the kitchen was the buttery, a room where drink was traditionally stored. In the Hawes' buttery were seven half, and three whole, hogsheads presumably containing home-brewed beer and ale. In the nearby larder there were wooden dishes, troughs and platters together with a large quantity of pewter. The platters, chargers, fruit dishes and plates, pie dishes, saucers (for sauce), porringers (for soup), and 12 spoons, all of pewter, would have been used every day for meals. There were also basins and ewers for washing the hands prior to eating, salt cellars, candlesticks, and five chamber pots, all of pewter. The Hawes did have some silver but this is not itemized.

Beyond this domestic area, and almost certainly arranged around a courtyard where the well was situated, was the dairy, and a whole range of other outbuildings; 'the malt howse, the yeeling howse, the kilne howse, the boulting howse, the brewhouse, the garner howse, the workhowse'. The dairy contained milk pans and butter and cheese-making utensils. Above the dairy was the cheese chamber where cheese and butter were stored, together with a tod (= 28 lbs) of wool, hurden yarn, a stone of tallow, various old implements and four flitches of bacon. This odd mixture of items, not at all unusual at this period, were probably stored together because the room was cool and airy.

In the Tudor and Stuart period large households in the country were fairly self-contained, living off their home-grown produce — milk, butter, cheese, flour, bread, ale, beer, meat, bacon, wool and yarn. The enormous amount of work required to produce these items was carried out in the separate houses or workshops. Malt for brewing was made in the kiln-house and malt-house, the brewing taking place in the 'yeeling howse' and brew-house. Threshed corn was stored in the garner-house and after being ground by the miller was sieved and prepared for use in the boulting-house. In this room were stored wooden tubs, troughs, sieves, measures and querns. Also the bread making utensils — moulding and kneading troughs, peels for lifting the bread from the oven — and two 'bucking loomes' or washing buckets. Meat was salted in a powdering tub or smoked in a smoke-cupboard in the chimney, and stored for the winter by hanging from hooks in dry places in the house. Wool was prepared from the fleeces and spun ready for weaving, similarly flax was prepared by retting and combing, then spun into linen yarn on the several spinning wheels about the house. Feathers in a tub, standing near the entry to the well court, were probably in preparation for new pillows and mattresses.

In the work-house were kept small tools and agricultural implements, for William Hawes was a farmer, if not on a very grand scale by the time of his death. He kept horses, cows, a bull, sheep, pigs, geese and hens, and during his last summer had grown rye, oats, barley, peas and 'about 40 loades of hay beinge verie badd', which was stored in three barns. In addition to the domestic outbuildings there were barns, carthouses, pigstys, cowsheds, and stables.

At the end of Hawes' inventory is listed the linen, of which there was a considerable quantity: 12 tablecloths, 20 towels, 11 pair pillowcases, 14 cupboard cloths, 12 dozen napkins and 26 pair of sheets of three qualities, flaxen (the best), hempen, and hurden (the coarsest).

William Hawes was buried in Solihull parish church, in St. Thomas' chapel, close to his father and a young grandson. In his will he stated that his wife, Ursula, was to stay at Hillfield Hall if she wished, having 'the chamber where she lyeth, the middle chamber, and the maides chamber adjoyninge' with the free use of other necesssary rooms, the household utensils, and the garden and orchard. His daughter, Constance, was left £300 to be paid in instalments, the first £100 being paid when she married or reached 24 years of age. His married daughters, Elizabeth and Ursula, were bequeathed various household goods. Edmund, his only surviving son, already had the land, and his legacy included certain pieces of furniture, some brewing vessels, all the maps and books in the house and the desk in the study. To his son-in-law, William Sheldon, his brother-in-law Michael Cole, his nephew Humphrey Cole, and his friend Reginald Brown he left 10s. each or a gold ring of that value. Mrs. Hawes, however, preferred to leave Hillfield; she exchanged houses with Edmund and moved to Shelly where she lived in domestic comfort until her death in 1615. As Edmund and his wife ultimately had at least 11 children, this was a sensible move.

A fine memorial to William and Ursula was placed in St. Thomas' chapel. It shows the figure of a man and a woman kneeling with eight children beside them. Elsewhere in the church is their Latin epitaph, the initial letters of which form an acrostic spelling GULIELMUS HAVVES (William Hawes). The final bill for the grave of William and Ursula, 13s. 4d. (36½p.) was paid in 1618.

Edmund Hawes had completed his move to Hillfield by October 1612 when his son, Edmund, was born and he remained there until his death in 1656. He took his part, as a gentleman, in the life of Solihull and the church. He was a Feoffee of the Charities collecting the parish rents and helping to administer the extensive properties which they owned. He and his wife had seats in the church, as did all those who could afford them, for which they paid a rent of 4d. (1½p.) per annum. Those who could not pay, had to stand during the services, presumably at the back of the church.

In 1604 Edmund and his lawyer cousin, Humphrey Cole had bought the lordship of the manor of Solihull from Thomas Throckmorton for £1,080. They did not retain it for long, however, and sold it to Samuel Marrow of Berkswell.

In 1635 Edmund Hawes' son, Edmund, sailed for America aboard the ship 'James' and settled in the town of Duxbury, near Boston, Massachusetts, thus founding the American branch of the Hawes family. Other Hawes are said to have moved to Staffordshire. On the death of Edmund, senior, Hillfield passed, via his sister, Ursula, to Sir Ralph Bovey, who was a nephew of her husband. Sir Ralph did not keep the property, selling it in the 1660's to George Feilding and his wife, Mary.

The Hawes Memorial in Solihull parish church.

The Feildings at Hillfield

George Feilding, a member of the aristocratic Denbeigh family, was described as 'a gentleman of about four or five hundred [pounds] a year'. He and Mary were newcomers to Solihull when they bought Hillfield Hall and the attached estate, having at some time previously lived at 'Ryegate' in Surrey, and at Berkswell. The estate when they acquired it consisted of five farms totalling 455 acres in all: Hillfield Hall and farm of 87 acres; Shelly Farm of 145 acres; Twist Farm of 22 acres; Pratts Farm of 21 acres, and an unnamed farm of 150 acres, plus a few other fields totalling 30 acres. In 1670 Feilding sold Shelly Farm to John Doley of Westminister the residual estate then being of 310 acres.

The Feildings seem to have altered Hillfield Hall almost immediately, apparently adding a whole new wing behind and adjoining the gatehouse front. In order to make room for this erection it was probably necessary to remove some, if not all, of the earlier service rooms; it was perhaps at this time that the stables and other outbuildings were moved to the present site.

Exactly what the new wing, which faced south east, looked like is unknown, but it is said to have been in the Italianate style with brick pillars or pillasters which had stone capitals; the design is reputed to have been by Inigo Jones. The Feilding family arms, later found in a Victorian part of the house, may have been placed on the new building at its completion. Carved in stone, they consisted of a shield bearing a spread eagle with a garter inscribed with the words 'Mon Espoier est en Dieu' — 'My hope is in God'. A new entrance, along a drive which opened into Widney Manor Road, was made and the garden, almost certainly, laid out formally, in the fashion of the day. In effect the house had been turned round leaving the out-moded Elizabethan gatehouse facade intact, but at the back of the house. The new front was elegant, with stylish sunny rooms looking over the garden, the country, and the drive, to the distant entrance gate.

George Feilding appears to have settled quickly into the life of Solihull, taking his share of duties in town and parish affairs. In 1671 he was elected the Parish Bailiff, but unfortunately before his year of office was completed, in March 1672, he died very suddenly. His wife and son, Robert, attempted to clear up his accounts, over which, in view of the suddenness of his death, there was some dispute. In April they attended a meeting to present the accounts: out of the parish money in hand Mr. Feilding had paid 12s.6d. (62½p.) for a Common Prayer Book and 2s.6d. (12½p.) for binding it; £2.3s.0d. (£2.15p.) to one Busby for 41 days work 'about the parish houses', and 16s. (80p.) to the sawyers for 16 days work. A balance of £12.10s.1d. (£12.50½p.) remained, of which Mrs. Feilding was allowed to keep £11.12s.0d. (£11.60p.) this being the cost of a silver gilt communion cup and cover which her husband had purchased on behalf of the parish. The cup, and the cover — 7 ins. in diameter with a button top — which can be used as a paten, are still owned by the church, although they are not in regular use.

After her husband's death, Mrs. Feilding remained at Hillfield, her son Robert, then about 20 years of age being a student at Queen's College, Oxford. In July 1672 he matriculated and the following year went to London to the Middle Temple to study law. George Feilding appears to have been a country gentleman content to run his estate and play his part in local affairs; his elder son, Robert, was a different sort of person altogether.

'Beau' Feilding.

Robert 'Beau' Feilding

At the time that Robert Feilding went to London the morals of the Court of Charles II and the town were very low, both being full of libertines and loose women. John Evelyn in his *Diary* continually deplored the behaviour of the Court which was set such a bad example by the King. It was not surprising, therefore, that Feilding, a good looking and seemingly charming young man, possibly finding his studies dry and tedious, should be attracted to its glitter. It is said that he 'drew nearer the Court living for some time in Scotland Yard'. He was soon noticed by King Charles who called him 'Handsome Feilding' and showed him favour by appointing him a Justice of the Peace for Westminster. Abandoning his studies Feilding became a courtier, the soubriquet 'Handsome' or as he was more usually called 'Beau' bringing him to the attention of several ladies of the King's entourage. Ever bold, he 'made his addresses to them and finding greater profit accruing to him than by being a Justice, he layd aside that office and gave himself wholly up to love and wine'.

Robert Feilding was a great success at Court and became notorious for his love affairs. He was frequently involved in fracas, but because as a gentleman he carried a sword, he usually came off best. All his life he seems to have been quick to draw and strike, often causing innocent people to suffer as a result. In 1677 he was pardoned by the King for manslaughter but who he killed is not known. Shortly after this he appears to have become an officer in the army. In 1681 Feilding attempted, unsuccessfully, to become the Member of Parliament for Coventry, standing as the Court party candidate.

Feilding's life style was extravagant and expensive; Jonathan Swift, thought that he had 'squandered' the property he acquired when he married Mary, the daughter of Barnham Swift, Viscount Carlingford. Unfortunately, Mary did not live long, and some time after 1684 'Beau' married again. His second wife was also named Mary; she was the only daughter of the Marquis of Clanricarde, and had been married twice before. Her first husband, Lord Muskerry, was killed at sea in 1665 and her second husband, Viscount Purbeck, was killed in a duel in 1684. Robert Feilding certainly moved and married in high social circles.

In February 1685 Charles II died; Robert remained at Court to become a favourite of the new King, James II. He began his service with James via the army in Warwickshire; in June 1685 Feilding was commissioned as a Captain of an independent troop of horse, and in 1688 was a Major in Lord Brandon's regiment of horse. It is said that 'Beau' also raised a regiment in Warwickshire for King James, he himself being its Colonel. In September 1685 Feilding became a Justice of the Peace for Warwickshire and remained so until 1688; he was Deputy Lieutenant of Warwickshire in 1686 having been put in the Commissions of the Peace for both Warwickshire and Middlesex the previous year. A royal bounty of £500 was given to him from the Privy Purse in 1685. In return for the King's interest in him 'Beau' became a Catholic and when James left England and fled to Ireland, Feilding followed him and was consequently outlawed by the new King and Queen, William III and Mary.

In Ireland 'Beau' sat in the Parliament of 1689, but by 1690 both he and James were in Paris where the ex-King settled down as a permanent exile. Such a life did not suit Feilding who preferred to live in England. He sued for a pardon, but did not succeed in getting one until 1695. The following year he returned to England as Major-General Feilding, and was at once in trouble, £200 being offered for his apprehension for assaulting and wounding a Justice of the Peace of Middlesex. He ended up as a prisoner in Newgate Gaol from which, however, he somehow managed to extricate himself.

Mary, Feilding's second wife had died in 1698, but with or without a wife he continued his amorous affairs, some of his lady friends paying him a handsome pension when the association ended.

Robert Feilding was satirized by Swift, and by Steele in *The Tatler*, not only for his licentious escapades but also for his swiftness with a sword 'running through a poor link boy to save the charge of lighting him home'; his meanness in failing to pay his tailor's bill and in dressing his footmen in black sashes made out of old mourning hat-bands; and his vainness and foppish dress, for he wished to be different and for people to notice him. When walking in the Mall he is reputed to have asked his footman whether his sword touched his right heel, and whether the ladies ogled him. On being told 'yes', 'Beau' replied, 'Let them die for love and be damned'.

In the early years of the new century Feilding was in his 50's, hard up as ever and conspicuous to the outside world, if not to himself, as an outdated remnant of Charles II's Court. He decided to marry again and looked around for a suitable lady with money. He promised £500 to a Mrs. Villars if she could arrange for him to marry a Mrs. Deleau, a widow with a fortune of £60,000. Mrs. Villars, who was Mrs. Deleau's hairdresser, agreed to arrange a meeting. However, she contrived to pass off another women, Mary Wadsworth, who was described as 'a jilt of the town' under Mrs. Deleau's name. 'Beau' was so keen to get hold of the fortune that he was quite deceived and when he went to his second meeting with the supposed Mrs. Deleau he took along a Catholic priest and they were married. Thus through this deceit, on 9th November 1705 the penniless Mary Wadsworth became Mrs. Feilding.

Simultaneously 'Beau' had been courting another lady, Barbara Castlemaine, the Duchess of Cleveland, once the mistress of Charles II. The Duchess was born in 1641, the daughter of William Villiers, Viscount Grandison. She married, in 1659, Roger Palmer who was later created Earl of Castlemaine, and the following year met King Charles and became his mistress. She had five children by the King, their three sons later being created the Dukes of Cleveland, Grafton and Northumberland.

Undoubtedly a great beauty, Lady Castlemaine was a greedy, avaricious schemer; she meddled in politics and intrigued against Lord Clarendon, the Lord Chancellor. Grossly extravagant she received gifts of jewels, money and plate of enormous value from the King. In 1670 she was created Duchess of Cleveland and given Nonesuch Park near Cheam in Surrey. Despite gifts, grants and settlements she was unable to afford her expensive lifestyle and disregarding historical associations dismantled Nonesuch Palace and sold its contents. She had many other lovers beside the King, and two other children, but none by her husband.

'Beau' Feilding and Barbara Castlemaine must have been old acquaintances with many common memories of Charles II and his Court. Although she was, no doubt, still attractive it was probably her wealth which drew Feilding to her. Only 16 days after his marriage with Mary Wadsworth, on 25th November 1705, he and the Duchess were married at St. James, Westminster.

Feilding was a bad husband to both his wives; incensed to discover that Mary Wadsworth was not Mrs. Deleau and the heiress he had supposed her to be, 'Beau' beat and bullied her. Barbara Castlemaine fared no better; he made free with her money, swore at her, drew his sword and threatened to kill her, and continued 'to riot with lewd women'. His stormy life with Barbara was brief, for in July 1706 Feilding was committed to Newgate for a short period for maltreating the Duchess. Mary Wadsworth, either from spite or for reward, then told the Duke of Grafton, the Duchess's grandson, that she too was Feilding's wife. Thereupon matters moved swifty and 'Beau' was prosecuted for bigamy at the Old Bailey.

His defence was that he did not think his marriage to Mary Wadsworth was legal as it was performed in a private house by a Catholic priest. He also said that he believed she already had a husband living; but it was 'plainly proved that he was married to them both'. He was found guilty and committed to the Fleet prison, but pardoned and 'escaped the punishment of burning in the hand'. Feilding's marriage with the Duchess was proved to be null and void and in May 1707 she went back to her old life.

'Beau' was like a pricked balloon; his foppishness vanished, his house was shut up and 'he made no more tours in a Calash through London all day long, that the Citizens might view his vanity'. He disappeared from the playhouse, the chocolate houses, coffee houses and taverns, and 'the most notorious rake of his time' was soon forgotten. Feilding had sold Hillfield Hall in 1705 and no longer had that to fall back on, but somehow or other he compounded with his creditors and paid off his debts. He may have gone abroad, to Holland, for a time, but when he died in 1712 aged 61, he was living with Mary Wadsworth, who had remained with him as his wife, in Scotland Yard.

Whilst Robert Feilding was living his dissolute life in London his mother continued to live at Hillfield. In 1683 she leased part of the estate, including part of the house, to Nicholas Rider of Solihull for £35 per annum. For her own use Mary Feilding retained 'all the new building and the rooms called the Greate Parlour and the room over against the Greate Parlour and Mr. Feilding's study in the old building'. She also retained 'the seat in the parish church belonging to the house'. Whether, during these years Feilding spent much time at Hillfield is unknown, but he was hardly the sort of man who would have cared to stay long in rural Solihull.

In March 1705 Robert Feilding (described as Major-General in the deed) sold Hillfield Hall and the estate to Henry Greswold of Solihull; it still consisted of 310 acres of land which was let to six tenants.

The Greswold Family at Hillfield

Henry Greswold was the son of the Rev. Henry Greswold, the rector of Solihull from 1660 to 1700, and the younger brother of Humphrey Greswold who built Malvern Hall. About the time that he bought Hillfield Henry married Jane Aston, they had six children and lived at the Hall throughout their married life. In 1743 Greswold added 20 acres of land to the estate by buying five fields called Sedgeleys; they lay to the south east of Whitefields Road and are now being developed for housing.

Henry Greswold died in 1749 leaving the Hall and land to his unmarried daughter, Ann. She died in 1756 all her property passing to her cousin, Mary Greswold, who had also inherited Malvern Hall where she lived with her husband, David Lewis. From this time Hillfield remained in the possession of the Greswold family as part of the Malvern Hall estate, the house being used, by the resident tenant farmer, as a farmhouse for about a century.

The tenant in 1795 was Peter Wooldridge who rented the farm land round the Hall plus Sedgeleys and three meadows, totalling 114 acres, for £105 per annum, as a yearly tenant. The Greswolds retained the right to 'hunt, set fowl with guns, dogs and hounds at all times but not to damage any corn or main crop'. Wooldridge was not permitted to grow flax, hemp or rape seed, which took a great deal out of the soil, and he was to provide 'two fowls or turkeys every New Years Day and must carry two loads of coal from New Caledonian Wharf each year' presumably for use at Malvern Hall.

In 1805 Stephen Sprigg took the tenancy of Hillfield Hall and the land on the same terms as Wooldridge. The Sprigg family remained at the Hall, farming this and other land belonging to the Malvern Hall estate for about 50 years. Miss Ann Sprigg was the tenant in 1851, but by 1861 she had left, and the house was empty. Possibly the farm was no longer a viable unit, for the London — Birmingham railway line, opened in 1852, had sliced through the Hillfield fields, splitting the farm and severing the entrance drive.

During its years as a farmhouse the Elizabethan gatehouse facade of the Hall had been defaced by unsightly additions and lean-to's which obliterated some windows. Those that remained looked out onto a farmyard surrounded by barns and outbuildings. A drawing by A.E. Everitt, an accomplished Birmingham artist, shows the house as it was in 1853. Mr. F.E. Greswolde Williams, who through his wife was the owner of the house in the 1860's, removed these accretions, 'modernised' the interior and made the gatehouse facade, once again, the entrance front of the house.

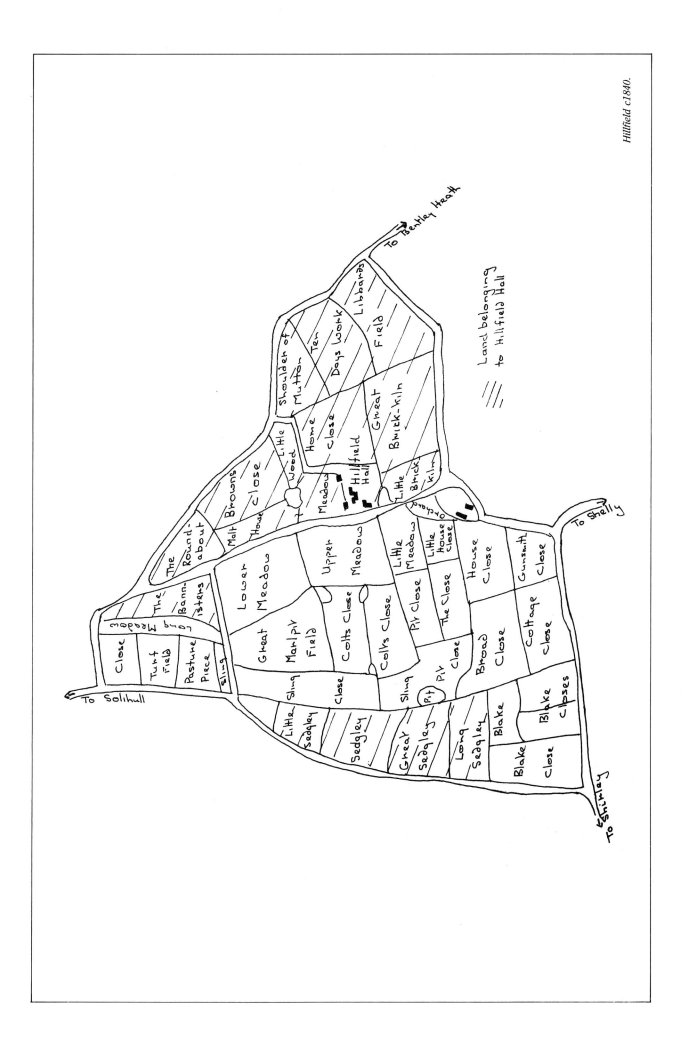

Hillfield c1840.

Hillfield Hall in 1853.

Unfortunately in January 1867, there was a disasterous fire at the Hall. Due to a heavy frost the Fire Engine had difficulty in reaching the house, the horses slipping on the icy roads; on arrival the men found the water for the hoses was frozen. As a result the south front of the Hall was virtually destroyed.

Hillfield was once again restored, but the elegant Stuart additions made by the Feildings were gone, Victorian rooms replacing them. By 1871 the house was occupied by George Beard, a pin and needle manufacturer, his wife and daughter; one of the many new families moving into Solihull at this time. They lived most comfortably with a staff of six, including a butler. The Beards remained in the house for many years and were succeeded by similar tenants.

In 1932 the Eveson family bought the Hall and removed some of the Victorian work carried out after the fire. When they sold the house in 1964 the accommodation consisted of a reception hall, drawing room, dining room, five bedrooms, kitchen, bathrooms, and domestic offices; the top floor — the original long gallery — was regarded as storage space. There were, by this time, only seven acres of ground with the house. Following the sale Hillfield Hall ceased to be a private house and became a night-club, the owner living in the fine spacious rooms on the first floor.

In 1974 the Hall was converted into a restaurant; prior to the opening a major restoration, including many alterations and additions took place. At the front of the house the entrance door was moved from the north to the west turret which had previously housed the spiral staircase. On the south side a large extension was built to contain the pleasant dining room and the kitchens. The marriage of the new building with the old was carried out sympathetically and tastefully and was so successful that the architects were given a Civic Trust Award.

THE FORGOTTEN HAMLET OF SHELLY

The area known as Shelly lies close to the Monkspath section of the Birmingham to Stratford-upon-Avon road two miles south of Solihull town. It is encompassed on the east by Widney Manor, on the south by the River Blythe, on the west by the Stratford Road and on the north by Shirley and Hillfield. Recently a new and very large housing estate, described as a mini-town, has been built. Covering much of Hillfield, Monkspath and Widney Lane it is now extending over Shelly. Ancient lanes have been closed and diverted and new roads built, completely altering the landscape.

Shelly Farm c.1920.

The Natural Landscape

Situated on a plateau some 130 metres high the land slopes gently southwards to the River Blythe which lies at approximately 122 metres O.D. Several small streams cross the area before draining into the Blythe which, in this section, has always been inclined to flood. One small tributary, which rises in Kettle Meadow beside Shelly Lane, formed a part of the boundary between the old parish of Solihull and that of Tanworth-in-Arden, Shelly being in both parishes.

The underlying rock is Keuper Marl which produces a heavy clay soil. However it is overlaid by large patches of drift, deposited by the melt waters of the ice age glaciers. The drift is made up of largish patches of sand and gravel and of boulder clay; alluvium along the river valley and the sides of the streams, plus an area of glacial lake deposit (laminated clay and silt). In places along the river bank, and where the Keuper Marl outcrops, the soil is unrewarding but on the lighter drift soil, on the higher ground back from the river, the soil would have been fairly easy to work. It is not surprising, therefore, to discover from documentary sources that a considerable community lived around Shelly in the post-Conquest period.

The Medieval Settlement

There is no evidence to show when the settlement at Shelly was founded but the earliest form of the name *Scelvesleia* meaning 'a clearing on a ledge of land on a river bank' suggests that it was perhaps established before the Conquest. The first recorded reference to Shelly is found in a deed of the third quarter of the 12th century in which William de Beaumont, the third Earl of Warwick (1153-84) granted the manor of Monkspath, adjoining Shelly to the south and west, to Roger de Ulehale of Tanworth, together with other land in the district.

A collection of 13th and 14th century deeds show that Shelly was a thriving settlement at that time. Traffic between Solihull and Henley-in-Arden passed through regularly, for Shelly Lane was then part of the Kings Highway, that is the main route between the two market towns. The road went via Church Hill, Hillfield, Shelly Lane and Shuttecotte Lane, then joined the Stratford Road at Monkspath Bridge. The bridge, probably a foot bridge only, is first recorded in 1339; previously there was a ford. From here, via Hockley Heath, the route was direct to Henley.

Several families, those of Brabasun, le Large, Whyte, de Shelleye, le Cras, de Yerdeley, Elys, Dercot, Faber, Crouenhale and Suansdich, are recorded as living in Shelley from 1250 onwards. Initially the land was farmed communally in selions or strips, deeds of the 13th century recording the gift of selions to Robert Brabisun by Thomas le Large. Later the land was enclosed and divided into severalty farms but the probable remnants of the open fields, in the form of ridge and furrow, were still to be seen in Graves Shelly Field in the 1960's. Some evidence of house platforms in Marl Pit Close possibly indicate part of the original settlement site, especially as this field adjoined an ancient trackway, once a continuation of Hay Lane, which led to Shelly Coppice. Hay Lane was also an ancient roadway making a cross roads with Shelly Lane.

Just south of the cross roads lay Gooseford Lane, a clearly defined medieval lane between banks and the continuation of the boundary between Solihull and Tanworth parishes; in the Archer Survey of Tanworth, taken in 1500, it is called 'the Narroo lone'.

Shelly Coppice (now partly destroyed) was a well established wood in the 15th century. In 1551 the trees were chopped down and the ground cleared so that it might be used for arable crops. By the 18th century it was restored to woodland and has remained so until recently when it was cut through by the M42. It had a very distinct bank and ditch which was probably dug to define and protect it and may have dated from its medieval establishment as a wood. From the southern centre of the Coppice ran Timber Lane which led across the Blythe towards Bentley Heath.

A watermill known as Swansditch and spelt variously Swannesdyke, Swaneditch, and Suansdich is known to have existed on the Blythe from 1240. References to the mill cease before 1500 and the exact situation of the mill building has never been firmly established. However it is thought to have been close to where Tellewelle Brook, flowing from the south east, from the direction of Box Trees, joins the Blythe. Here a leet shows the area of the mill if not its actual site. The family of Swansditch worked the mill in the 13th and 14th century, but they were leasing it to others in 1340. The mill pool was also used as a fish pool.

Commercial fish pools were a thriving business in the medieval period when the church decreed so many meatless days. There were many fish pools in Tanworth as well as Swansditch Mill and there was fishing in the river; from 1332 there was also Smiths Pool at Shelly. This pool was created by John Fabro (Smith) of Monkspath from 'an open ditch' granted to him by Roger de Middleton of Tanworth. The pool was situated south of Gooseford Lane on a larger and more important tributary of the Blythe than that which formed the Solihull/Tanworth boundary. It flowed from the west through fields later called Broom Meadow and Broomfield, Shelly Lane, to the east of the pool, crossing over the dam. The pool changed hands frequently and was obviously a valuable property. Its banks were clearly visible until the 1970's and the outlet on the north side of the dam, by Shelly Lane, was still working.

Just past the dam the medieval Kings Highway bent sharply and changed its name from Shelly Lane to Shuttecotte (Short cut) Lane. Following an earlier and lesser way Shelly Lane continued, straight, to the river. It crossed the Blythe by a ford at the end of the mill leet before continuing as Mulne Lane, to join Gate Lane. It was probably the making of Munkespathe Brugg (Monkspath Bridge) avoiding the ford, which caused the 'short cut' to become the main route for through traffic.

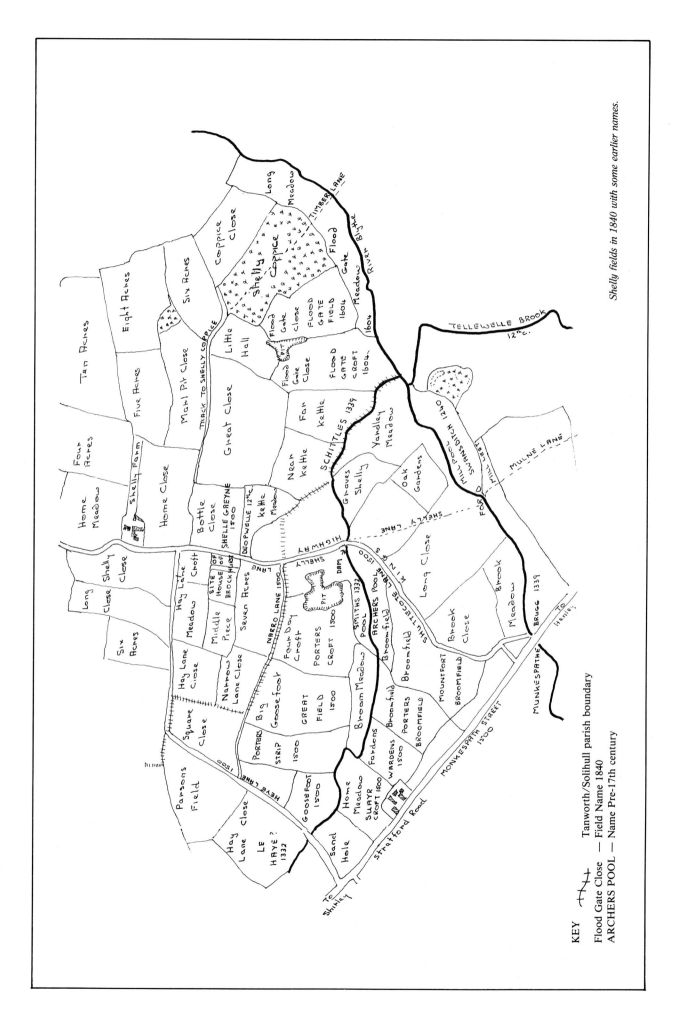

KEY

Flood Gate Close — Field Name 1840

ARCHERS POOL — Name Pre-17th century

Tanworth/Solihull parish boundary

Shelly fields in 1840 with some earlier names.

51

The deed of 1332 recording the establishment of Smiths Pool makes reference to Le Haye which was adjacent. The name *haye* means 'fenced-in piece of ground', 'an enclosure'. In a hedgeless open field settlement such as Shelly seems to have been originally, an area enclosed by a fence or hedge, whatever its purpose, would have been a prominent feature of the landscape. Le Haye is thought to be the field called, in the 19th century, Hay Lane Close; rectangular in shape it measured just over eight acres. Hay Lane presumably takes its name from Le Haye.

A group of fields called Kettles which lie on the Solihull side of the boundary stream were known in the 14th century as Schittles which may be derived from the place-name element *skil* meaning 'a boundary'. John Fabro, who made Smiths Pool, was permitted by Walter de Suanesdich of the mill to take half the fish in the river between Schittles and the mill.

Another group of fields with appropriate names are those surrounding Shelly Coppice on the river side. They are called Floodgate, this being an area where the river is liable to flood and where gates were situated to control the water to the mill. John Fabro was allowed to take fish here too, 'half the fish coming to the gates called the Flodyaten' (Floodgates).

A further boundary mark mentioned in the grant of Monkspath manor was *deopwelle* meaning 'a spring or stream in a deep place'. This dark hole was at the side of Kettle Meadow near the boundary stream.

During the 14th century the land at Shelly appears to have been enclosed and held in severalty. Some of the long established family names disappeared: by 1359 the White family had died out, the remaining daughter, Sarah, who had married a Coventry man, selling their property in Shelly.

Deed material is scarce for the 15th century but it would seem that the community went into decline. The land was worked but by fewer people and the ownership was in the hands of non-residents. The names of the land holders in the Tanworth part of Shelly — Thomas Waring, John Porter, William Moor, Sir William Norres, Simon Montfort, John Archer, Thomas Hawes and the Guild of Henley — are revealed in the Archer Survey of 1500. By this date the mill had ceased working and Smiths Pool, now called Archers Pool, was no longer used as a fishery. The Solihull part of Shelly is less well documented but much of it appears to have been held by the Hawes family, the Brockhursts, the Warings and the Wheighalls.

The Hawes Family at Shelly and Shelly Farm

Richard Hawes the son of John Hawes of Solihull held houses and land in Shelly in 1366, but seems not to have been resident. By 1500 three members of the family had property in the hamlet, one of them, Thomas Hawes, being described as 'of Schelley'. Exactly where he lived is not stated but documentary evidence suggests that his home was on the site of Shelly Farm. The present farmhouse, recently converted to a public house, is thought to have been built by a later member of the Hawes family but the date of its construction was uncertain. However detailed monitoring and recording of the building, undertaken during the conversion work, has enabled the sequence of its development to be deduced.

The core of the present house was erected about 1590 — 1600. A two storey timber framed building, facing west, it originally consisted of two bays divided by an axially placed chimney stack, with a cross wing and porch on the north. The chimney provided back-to-back hearths heating each of the four main rooms; a hall to the north of the stack and a parlour to the south on the ground floor, and two bedrooms above. The front elevation was close studded, the vertical timbers being set close together above and below a central rail. The rear and the southern walls were close studded on the ground floor with square panels above. Decorative wavy bracing was applied to the south gable-end. The cross wing and porch, also both of two storeys, adjoined the hall, twin doors in the north wall leading into the wing which contained service rooms. The porch, originally open below but with a small chamber above measuring internally 6ft.5ins. by 4ft.10ins., still stands at the north west corner of the building. It formed the main entrance and led directly into the hall.

The house was at this stage of its development when Edmund Hawes, the son of William Hawes of Hillfield Hall, moved in with his wife and four children in 1607. They remained at Shelly Farm until 1611 when William Hawes died. Edmund then exchanged houses with his mother, Ursula, he moving to Hillfield Hall and she to Shelly Farm where she lived until her death in October 1615.

Mrs Hawes by her will made in March 1614 left 40s. (£2) to the poor of Solihull; a bed complete with bolster, pillows, sheets and blankets plus other linen, to her grand-daughter Jane, and her 'damaske gowne' and a pair of 'flanderes' candlesticks to her daughter-in-law. Her daughter, Elizabeth was to have her wedding ring; her daughter, Ursula a 'silver spoone' and William, her grandson, £5 and his grandfather's ring. There were other bequests to family and friends including 37 books, valued at 25s.4d. (126½p.) and agricultural implements to Edmund. Her unmarried daughter, Constance, who lived with her, received the residue of her estate.

An inventory of Mrs. Hawes goods lists the rooms at Shelly Farm: hall, parlour, buttery, dairy, backhouse, kitchen and five bedrooms upstairs plus the closet — the small room over the porch — and their contents.

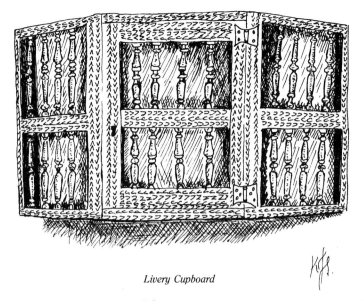

Livery Cupboard

The hall was furnished as a dining room, the cooking at Shelly, as at Hillfield, being carried out in the kitchen. The parlour was used only as a sitting room, and was cosily furnished with chairs, stools, a livery cupboard, and a pair of little tables. As at Hillfield there were needlework cushions, a screen to keep draughts away and two footstools to lift the ladies' feet off the floor. There were carpets for decoration and curtains at the window.

The stairs were probably situated to the west of the chimney, between the hall and the parlour. They ascended directly into the room above, 'the chamber over the parlour'. This contained two wooden bedsteads both hung about with curtains, those at the head of one bed being arranged to resemble a tent. Only one bed was used and this had, in addition to the bed clothes, a silk valance and silk cushions. The room was quite full for it also held a chest, a trunk, chairs, stools, a cupboard, and a settle. There were curtains at the window and a hearth furnished with andirons and bellows. It is not clear whether Mrs. Hawes slept in this room or that adjoining which was over the hall.

The hall chamber contained a large bed with a small truckle bed under it. The truckle, usually slept in by a servant or a child, was pulled out at night and pushed away in the day time. This room was also full of furniture for there were two chests, a box, a twig chair with two cushions, a cupboard, stools, a press — an early type of wardrobe — and two coffers of cypress wood. A large piece of panelling or wainscott suitable 'for a closet' was also in the room.

The three other bedrooms, reached by a back stair, were in the north wing above the service rooms. They were furnished more simply, generally with a bed and some sort of storage for clothes. They were probably occupied by the servants.

The closet, over the porch, was entered from the service wing and contained Mrs. Hawes most valuble possessions — a salt cellar, a jug, two bowls, seven spoons, all of silver — valued at £10. The room also contained a coffer, 'a tub to keep pewter in', a small black box and some drinking glasses including four from Venice.

In the service wing, which was probably of at least three bays, were the back stairs, the buttery, the kitchen, the dairy and the backhouse. The buttery contained barrels, a hogshead, two 'frames to sett hogsheads upon', wooden vessels and a large quantity of pewter. There were five dozen trenchers (wooden plates), a chafing dish for heating food at the table, and several bottles, of leather, pewter and twiggen, for carrying drink on journeys and to the fields. In the backhouse were stored brewing and bread making utensils, and in the dairy milk vessels and cheese making equipment, although Mrs. Hawes kept no cows, only a horse, a pig and some poultry.

The last room to be described in the inventory was the kitchen. This contained little furniture apart from two wooden screens, perhaps to shield the cooking fire from draughts, and a dresser where the food was prepared. There were, however, numerous cooking utensils — 'kettles, posnetts, frying pannes, driping pannes, brasse potts, a brasse pan' — together with four pot hangers, a pair of pothooks and an iron bar fixed in the chimney. There was a pestle and mortar for grinding spices and a salt coffer close to the fire.

Mrs. Hawes had a large quantity of linen including 23 pairs of sheets, 12 tablecloths, 15 towels and 8¾ dozen napkins — the latter were needed to wipe the fingers at table, for as yet forks were not used, only knives, spoons and fingers. The linen valued at £28 was probably stored in the cypress chests. Ursula Hawes clothes were valued at £50, a considerable sum

Chest

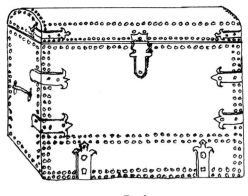

Trunk

for the period.

Outside in the barn, the core of which has been made into a Bar and restaurant during the recent conversion, was a small quantity of oats and hay, and in the stable the horse with its saddle and other equipment.

Press

In 1604 the Hawes, William, Ursula and Edmond, had sold a close in Shelly called Dipwell Grove, of 13 acres extent, to Thomas Brockhurst for £110. This and three other smaller fields appear to have been close to the Solihull/Tanworth boundary and were adjoined on the north by other land of the Hawes. In 1616 Edmund Hawes leased Dipwell (Deepwell) Grove and other land back to Brockhurst for 200 years. Also included was the house where Brockhurst lived: this was possibly situated in Shelly Lane between Gooseford Lane and Hay Lane, on the opposite side of the road to Shelly Farm. However, by 1647 Dipwell Grove and the other fields leased in 1616 were in the hands of Oliver Whigham, who was passing them into the possession of Henry Averell of Olton.

Throughout this period the Hawes continued to own Shelly Farm and probably other land in Shelly. When Edmund died in 1656 his property passed to Sir Ralph Bovey who sold the Hillfield estate to George Feilding in the 1660's. In 1670 Feilding sold Shelly Farm to John Doley of Westminster.

Shelly 1670 — 1885

The history of Shelly in Tanworth from this time onwards is not known but the Archer family of Umberslade appear to have owned it for a considerable period. Similarly there are few references to Shelly in Solihull in the 17th and 18th centuries although it is known that in 1789 Shelly Farm was occupied by William Smith and owned by Mr. Short. Some years later the Rate Book of 1806 records William Harding as the owner, William Smith still being the occupant.

It was probably during the tenancy of Mr. Smith that Shelly Farm was added to: a south wing of brick, two storeys high, being built against the old external wall of the parlour. The accommodation comprised a parlour to the front, a service room behind (later a dairy), with a bedroom at the front upstairs and a probable cheese room behind. At the same time the ground floor timbers of the external walls of the main range were replaced by brick and a new front door inserted. This was placed in its present position, in the centre of the west front. It opened into an entrance lobby formed by the chimney stack and the doors to the old parlour and the hall. The stairs which had been situated here were removed and a new staircase inserted against the west wall of the hall.

Some time after this the timber framed service wing was taken down leaving only the porch. A new kitchen was provided by adding a new wing behind the hall, at the north east of the house. Shelly farmhouse remained in this form until 1985 when work began to make it suitable for use as a public house.

Shelly generally appears to have become a quiet backwater, the roads passing through losing their former importance and gradually falling out of use. About 1820, when enclosure was being discussed, many little-used roads and lanes were closed. Amongst these were Shuttecotte Lane, Timber Lane and part of Shelly Lane, all of which were considered superfluous. However the Birmingham to Stratford road continued to be an important highway. In 1726 it was turnpiked and became one of the major routes between Birmingham, Oxford and London from this time until the advent of the motorway.

By 1840 Shelly Farm, then estimated at 135½ acres was owned by Thomas Heydon and occupied by Samuel

Matthews. Other Shelly landowners were Henry Greswold and Thomas Rose whose tenant, Thomas Bott, occupied a house possibly on the site of that of Thomas Brockhurst. Botts' house, Shelly Farm and a farmhouse on the Stratford Road between Hay Lane and Monkspath Bridge (referred to as a cottage in 1646) are the only three houses shown on the Tithe Map of c.1840. The area had changed hardly at all when the first edition of the 6″ Ordnance Survey map was made in 1885.

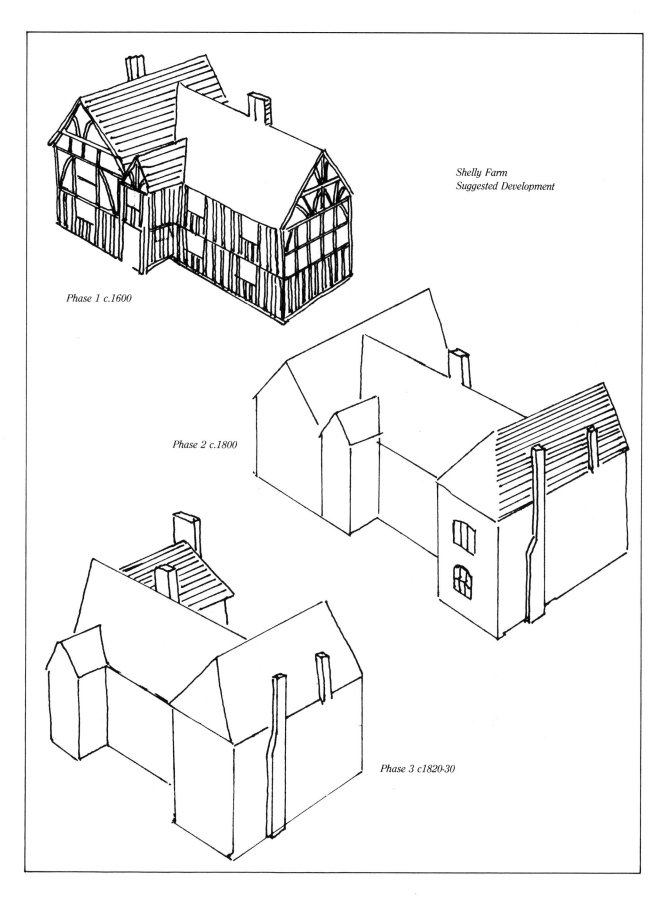

Shelly Farm
Suggested Development

Phase 1 c.1600

Phase 2 c.1800

Phase 3 c.1820-30

Modern Changes and Development

In the years since 1885 a great many changes have taken place at Shelly. In the 1930's a row of semi-detached houses was erected in Hay Lane and some years earlier several small houses were built at Shelly Green. Along the Stratford Road, between Hay Lane and Monkspath Bridge, further houses and one or two businesses, including a garden centre, have been established.

During the autumn of 1971 considerable drainage work was undertaken along the banks of the Blythe; the river meadows were disturbed but none of the higher ground. About the same time the proposed route of the M42 motorway was published, this led the Solihull Archaeological Group to walk the line of the road between Stratford Road and Copt Heath and to research its history. The motorway has now been built and has cut a swathe across the countryside obliterating some features within Shelly. Shelly Coppice has been sliced through and partially destroyed as have Mulne Lane, Swansditch mill pool and the Kettle Fields.

More recently the housing development has brought a multiplicity of new roads. Shelly Lane (part of which was latterly known as Hay Lane) has virtually disappeared and the older houses at Shelly Green are surrounded by new residences. Shelly Farm, which remained as an agricultural unit worked by a tenant until the early part of 1985, has been totally renovated, and altered to make it suitable for public use. In the main range the axial chimney stack has been removed and Mrs. Hawes' hall and parlour thrown into one large room, now the main Bar. The ground floor of the brick south wing remains as two separate rooms. A flat for the manager has been made on the upper floor of the building. The Brewery have added a brick extension on the north of the building and a glazed extension on the east. Many of the farm buildings have been demolished; the very large barn, however, has been completely stripped down, refurbished, and made into a spacious and attractive Bar. The popular entrance into the *Shelly Farm* is through the glazed east extension which leads from a large car park. The latter also serves the adjacent school and health centre, all of which are built on land previously the farm yard, The Pleck, Home Close and Home Meadow. Shelly which has been rural and quiet for so many centuries is once again a living settlement.

Rugby House, Warwick Road. Now the office of Roland Evans, solicitor, and previously part of a butcher's shop.

Silhill Hall which stood in Streetsbrook Road until 1966 when it was demolished illegally.

SOLIHULL FREE GRAMMAR SCHOOL

There is a tradition that a school existed in Solihull from the time of Richard II but there is no evidence to support this notion. The acknowledged date of the Free Grammar School's foundation is 1560 when the endowments, previously used to support the chantry chapels of St. Catherine and of St. Mary, were allocated to pay the salary of a schoolmaster. In 1566 the revenue of a third suppressed chantry, that of St. Alphege (and like the others situated in the parish church), was also assigned to the master's salary.

Malvern House, Park Road early this century.

The school, open to the sons of all the parishioners of Solihull, was administered by the Feoffees who also looked after the many other charity properties. The pupils were taught to read and write in English, but Greek and particularly Latin — Virgil, Ovid, and Latin verse and composition — were the major subjects. When they were between 14 and 18 years of age the boys might go to Oxford or Cambridge and then into the professions.

The schoolhouse was situated close to the church, in Park Road, in a timber framed building later known as Malvern House. It remained on the same site until 1882 although the original building was altered and added to over the centuries.

The Schoolmasters and the Buildings 1560 — 1705

The first master of the Grammar School was Edward Pole who received a salary of £2. per quarter in 1560 and after 1566 £12. per annum. He did not stay long at Solihull and was followed by a succession of masters, most of whom received a lower stipend.

In 1574 a Lower School was started for younger boys. The lessons, in English only, were taught by a second master or usher in the Grammar School building. In 1612 Barnaby Fetherston was paid '29s.8d. (148½p.) with 45s. (225p.) to come' for teaching the 'lyttell children' that is those in the Lower School.

A new headmaster, John Horne, was appointed in 1592. He remained at the school until his death in 1635 and during all his 43 years in the post his salary remained at £12. per annum. Horne almost certainly supplemented this by taking a number of boarders, boys who were not from Solihull and had therefore to pay for both their tuition and accommodation. During his time a considerable amount of building took place at the 'scholehous', £31.7s.0d. (£31.35p.) being expended in 1615 and £35.16s.0d. (£35.80p.) in 1629. Even so the building was not very large, as is shown by the inventory of Horne's goods taken after his death in November 1635. This records that the schoolhouse contained a parlour, hall, buttery, and schoolroom downstairs with four bedrooms above. The parlour, where Horne and his wife slept was also their sitting room. In addition to the bed there was a little table, four high and three low stools, a cupboard and a coffer. A bench provided further seating and there were five cushions.

The hall was more like a kitchen than a living room the bulk of the contents being cooking utensils and pewter table-ware. The kettles, pots and pans were all of brass and there was a brass basting ladle and a skimmer. A table, three chairs, three spinning wheels and some shelves were the only pieces of furniture in the room, but in the buttery were two benches and a form; perhaps these were brought out at meal times when the master, his wife, family and boarding pupils gathered together at table.

There can have been few boarders at the time of John Horne's death, for of the four rooms upstairs only two were furnished. The chamber over the parlour contained a bed, three stools, three desks, a little chair, a cupboard, a coffer, and all Horne's books, valued at £4.; this was nearly one seventh of the total value of his possessions. The next room contained two beds, three coffers, and a pair of trestles and a board, which if put together made a table. Also in this room were 20 lbs. of dressed hemp. The two rooms over the schoolroom contained only stored items, planks, yarn and 'certaine trumpery and old things'. The contents of the schoolroom are not recorded, for these belonged to the school and did not form part of Horne's estate.

On the schoolmaster's death Mrs. Horne had to leave the house but she remained in Solihull for a short while, sharing her pew in the church with three other ladies. Her husband had owned a copy of Cooper's *Dictionary* and this she sold to the Feoffees for 7s. (35p.), as they wished it 'to remaine in the schoole'.

John Horne was followed as master, in turn by Samuel Wilkes, James Horton, and John Makepeace, but none of them stayed long, indeed Makepeace left after six months. In 1658 Henry Biggs was appointed; he was the first master to receive a salary of £15. per annum. This was an attempt, perhaps, to persuade him to take fewer boarders and boys from outside the town, who may have been crowding out the Solihull pupils.

Biggs left after five years and the Feoffees decided that the next master should be offered a stipend of £20. per annum. But, six months later they appointed George Long at the enormous sum of £25. per annum. This large salary carried obligations and an agreement dated January 1664 was drawn up setting them out. Long was not to admit too many 'forrein children', not to take on any other business or employment, and to teach the boys to 'fitt them for the university'. He was also to keep the school buildings in repair, but as they were to be put in good order by the Feoffees first, Long seems to have struck a good bargain. William Blunt, who was the master of the Lower School (at a salary of £8. per annum) was to assist him,

'and it is our will and resolution that neither William Blunt nor any parents of any children that are or shall be taught in the free school shall have any liberty to quarrell with or contradict Mr. Long in anything'.

The proposed work on the schoolhouse included repairs to the buttery and parlour, plastering the walls where they needed it, mending the doors, the locks and providing new keys. The roof was to be re-tiled and all the windows re-glazed;

'and as soone as timber can be felled and sawd and the weather serve, to board the Parler floor and pargett [plaster] the parler chamber. And also to build a house of office [lavatory] upon the school land where Mr. Long shall appoint'.

Then, as now, school boys bumped and barged about, giving doors, walls and windows rough treatment.

As soon as the weather was suitable work began. Oliver Withies sawed planks and boards (charge 7s.8d. = 39p.) and a further 100 boards were purchased from Goodman Woodert (cost 8s.4. = 42p.). The roof needed 600 tiles, two crest tiles and four gutter tiles, which with carriage amounted to 12s.6d.(62p.). Richard Taylor supplied eight bunches of tiling laths for 6s.8d. (33p.). For the plastering and pargetting five quarters of lime were fetched from Walsall by Henry Wright (lime and carriage £1.) and four loads of clay and hair to mix with it were provided by Mr. Greswold. The work required more than 65 man days to complete: George Linold, his father and their men; Richard Sutton and his man; Robert Hardyman; Francis Riddell and Reginald Veale, all taking part and being paid wages of between 6d. (2½p.) and 1s. (5p.) each per day. The nails used in the building

'3,000 lath nails at 1s.8d. (8½p.) per thousand, for 1,000 more at 1s.5d. (7p.) and two pennyworth of 8d nails and one pennyworth of 6d. nails'.,

were bought from William Hows and together cost 7s.2d. (36p.).

The windows were glazed by John Lluellyn (cost £1.19s.9d. = £1.98p.), three locks were put on the doors (cost 1s.8d. = 8½p.) and a porch was built with planks which had been soaked in water, Rudgley Ward receiving 1s. (5p.) 'for drawing out of ye water ye planks' and delivering them to the schoolhouse. Finally on a morning when they 'did no other worke' three of the men 'raised' the lavatory; that is they put up the timber framed walls which had already been assembled on the ground. When the work was completed they celebrated by drinking ale provided by the Feoffees — the charge of 1s.6d. (7½p.) would have bought approximately four and half gallons.

After five years, his agreement having expired, George Long, left Solihull his place being taken by Jonathan Coove at a salary of £20. per annum. He agreed to keep the schoolhouse in repair, not to have more than 12 boarders, and with the assistance of William Blunt, to teach the children to 'write, reade, cast accounts, Latine and Greeke, as their parents shall request', the hours and days of school being stipulated —

'From Candlemas to St. Andrews Day [2nd February — 30th November]
7 a.m. — 11 a.m.   including Saturdays and except
1 p.m. — 5 p.m.   Thursdays when stop at 3 p.m.

St. Andrews Day to Candlemas
9 a.m. — 3 p.m.   with one hours play from 11 a.m. to noon.

Holidays — Holy Days
          From 2nd day before Easter and all Easter week
          From 2nd day before Whit and all Whit week
          From 9 days before Christmas and to the Monday following 6th January'

When Coove left in 1671 the next master, George Ward, was offered a salary of £28. per annum without an usher or £20. with one, and the house rent free. He tried without an assistant but found the work too much. In 1686 the Feoffees, being hard pressed for money, reduced his stipend to £13. a year, but restored it to £20. in 1687. They also paid the arrears of £20. which they owed him, and for the repairs which he had made to the school building. Although a fairly young man Ward died in March 1689 and his mother was paid the 47 weeks salary owing to him.

Josiah Foster of Birmingham was engaged as master in September 1689 at £13.10s.0d. (£13.50p.) per annum. However his appointment appears not to have been permanent, for every six months the agreement was renewed, his salary being raised to £25. for himself and an usher in September 1690.

A new master, William Hiron of Sutton-under-Brailes was appointed in 1691, but he was not to take up his post until April 1693. Hirons began teaching in Solihull as arranged, but he was not satisfactory and was dismissed in 1694. His usher, Samuel Osborne, was made the headmaster for the time being.

Osborne held the school together until January 1695 when John Hunter of Birmingham was engaged, to start immediately, at a salary of £28. with an usher. By December it was clear that he was eminently suitable and he was appointed for a further seven years at £22. per annum for himself, and £8. for the usher. He stayed at Solihull until 1705 when he resigned to become headmaster of Lichfield Grammar School where he taught Samuel Johnson.

A Fine Reputation

John Crompton followed Hunter and during his 30 years as master the school gained a fine reputation. His salary was to be £27. per annum and £8. for the usher; he was allowed to take boarders but should their number reach eight he was to forgo £7. of his salary.

Crompton gave his pupils an excellent classical education, amongst them was John Taylor, later a Greek scholar known as 'Demosthenes' Tayor; Christopher Wren of Wroxall, the grandson of the famous architect; and two minor poets, Richard Jago and William Shenstone.

Jago was born in 1715 at Beaudesert where his father was the rector; after leaving Solihull Grammar School he went to Oxford and was later a curate at Lapworth and vicar of Harbury and of Chesterton. In 1754 he was appointed vicar of Snitterfield where he remained until his death in 1781. His long poem *Edge Hill* describes, with many moral and other digressions, the views seen at morning, noon, afternoon and evening as he looks down from the famous hill over Warwickshire. In it he mentions Solihull, his schoolmaster and his friend, Shenstone.

After his school days, Shenstone also went to Oxford, to Pembroke College where he was a contemporary of Samuel Johnson. His later life was devoted to landscape gardening; to his estate at The Leasowes, Halesowen; to his poetry, criticized for 'artificial prettiness'; and to his circle of friends which included Lady Luxborough of Barrells Park, Ullenhall, local intellectual gentry and old school friends, including Jago.

When John Crompton left Solihull in 1735 for Market Bosworth Grammar School, Samuel Johnson applied for the post of master, but the Feoffees turned him down —

> 'The Feoffees all agree that he is an excellent scholar and upon that accound deserves much better than to be schoolmaster of Solihull. But then he has the caracter of being a very haughty, ill-natured gent, and yt he has such a way of distoring his fface (w^h though he cannot help) ye gent^n think it may affect some young ladds; for these two reasons he is not approved on, ye late master Mr. Crompton's huffing the ffeoffees being stil in their memory'.

instead the Rev. Richard Mashiter was appointed.

Mashiter was only 23 years of age and newly ordained. In 1742 he married Mary Holbech of Bentley Heath, the daughter of one of the Feoffees. He and his son Edward, who succeeded him, held the headship until 1781. Edward Mashiter died in office and was followed by Rev. James Eyre.

During the time of the Mashiters further extensive work was carried out to the school building. In 1744 £213.10s.4d. (£213.51½p.) was spent on repairs and 'making certain alterations and additional buildings'. The largest bills were for bricks and tile, boards, lime, 'timberwork' and masons and carpenters work. It has been estimated that in the region of 50,000 bricks were used during the work, and it was probably at this time that the building acquired its brick walls in place of the previous ones of timber framing. Mr. Mashiter was called upon to contribute £90.10s.4d. to the total cost, presumably because a good deal of the work was on the house in which he lived.

An almost annual expense for the Feoffees was repairing the windows of the school, presumably damaged by the activities of the boys, although a hailstorm was the cause in October 1783. The unpleasant task of cleaning out the boys' lavatory or 'necessary house' was undertaken in May 1752 by William Williams who was paid 6d. (2½p.) for the work. Subsequent payments for cleaning were recorded in October 1752, June 1754 and August 1754. It is to be hoped that it was cleaned out on other, unrecorded, occasions too.

James Eyre also married the daughter of a Feoffee, Charlotte Harding, her solicitor father, Judd, living in a house opposite the church. Eyre was a great friend of the famous Whig, Dr. Samuel Parr, vicar of Hatton, whose second wife was Eyre's sister.

In 1801 Parr described Eyre's life as a schoolmaster in a letter to Lord Chedworth —

> 'He has the care of a small country school, with a tolerable house and an annual salary of about £80. He was educated at Oxford. He is more than fifty years old. He has for many years served two curacies, very distant from each other, for a stipened which . . . amounts nearly to £60 a year . . . he has no chance of preferment. He is a very good scholar. He is a sensible man; his principles are honest; his application to books is extensive; and his conduct is quite irreprochable. He has an excellent wife and six children. With an income so scanty . . . it is utterly impossible for him to make the smallest provision for so numerous a family at his death . . . during the late season of distress [when bread prices were extremely high] he has found it difficult to procure food and raiment for the passing day'.

As a result of these words, Eyre was given the living of Winterbourne in Wiltshire, which helped his finances considerably. James Eyre, his family eventually increasing to ten children, continued to live and teach in Solihull until he died in 1813.

In 1812 it had been suggested that the Lower School be severed from the Grammar School, and a new separate school, more in line with contemporary teaching be established. John Powell, who was the master of the Lower School resigned, expecting to take charge of the new school. The scheme however, came to nothing and the two schools remained together until 1850. Powell, who had a private school of his own elsewhere in the village, did not return to the Lower School.

Following James Eyre's death an advertisement for a new headmaster was placed in various newspapers in Oxford, Cambridge, Birmingham, and Warwick.

'Wanted a Headmaster of the Free Grammar School of Solihull in Warwickshire. He must be a graduate of one of the Universities. The salary will be £100 per annum, with a house capable of receiving 18 or 20 boarders, and garden and croft containing 2 acres of land, clear of all taxes'.

The payment of the taxes by the Feoffees was a valuable perquisite, for during the Napoleonic wars these could amount to £12. a year on the school and schoolhouse.

The successful candidate was John Griffin who was to teach much the same syllabus as in 1669, school hours, however, were now shorter —

'From Michaelmas to Lady Day [29th September to 25th March]
9 a.m. — noon and 1 p.m. — 4 p.m.

The rest of the year
8 a.m. — noon and 2 p.m. — 5 p.m.

Holidays —   1 month at Christmas
1 month at Midsummer
1 week at Easter
2 half days each week'

The new second master, to replace John Powell, was Robert Cumber who was to have the large salary of £65. per annum. He supplemented this by supplying inkwells to the school, his charge for three inkwells being 10½d. (4p.). When Cumber resigned in 1840 his successor, Thomas Wood, brought new ideas. He asked if the schoolroom could be whitewashed, if the desks could be arranged differently and the windows made to open. He remained only a year, perhaps the outcome of his revolutionary demands!

Doldrums and Dissension

In 1828 the two schoolrooms, one used for the Grammar School and the other for the Lower School, had been enlarged and an extra upper room provided for the senior boys. John Griffin, in time, took over the upper room for his own use, and the reason why it was not needed for lessons became apparent in 1842 when an Act of Parliament for the improvement of Grammar Schools was passed. Looking at Solihull Grammar School in detail, it was discovered that the Upper School, taught by Griffin, had no free pupils, and indeed had never had more than three or four during all his 30 years as master. There were a few private boarding pupils, but the classical education offered was not attractive to most Solihull parents who wished their sons to learn more practical subjects than Latin and Greek. The Lower School, which offered the three R's plus religious instruction and simple geography, had 75 pupils of all ages, taught solely by Joseph Sice, the usher. John Griffin was receiving his salary, living rent free in the schoolhouse and taking over rooms left empty by a lack of pupils, but teaching no Solihull boys, only a few private boarding pupils whose fees were his prerogative. Meanwhile, in the adjoining room, Joseph Sice struggled alone with 75 boys.

The Feoffees suggested that the Grammar School syllabus be changed to include R.I., history, geography, composition, higher arithmetic and practical geometry, but Griffin objected to any changes and resigned. He was given a pension of £50. per annum. It is not surprising that the private schools, of which there were several in the village, were so successful.

Changes were made at the school; the suggested subjects were introduced and a basic test of admittance instituted. Boys had to 'be able to read English fluently, to write a fair hand and be conversant with the four first rules of arithmetic'. The post of headmaster was advertised at £100. per annum, the taking of 12 fee paying pupils at a charge not exceeding £50. per boarder, still being permitted. It took some time to attract a new man but at last Rev. George Elliott took over. In anticipation of an influx of new pupils the size of the Upper School was limited to 45 boys.

However, no free pupils joined the school. The people of Solihull now began to complain, for they believed that this new master too was being paid for doing nothing, in addition discipline throughout the school was bad. A great petition, several yards long and signed by hundreds of people, against the way the Grammar School was being conducted by the masters and managed by the Feoffees, was presented to them in March 1850.

As a result Sice was dismissed and Rev. Elliott resigned. Shortly afterwards the Lower School was moved to a new schoolroom, on the site of the present St. Alphege School, next to the church, and was henceforth called the Elementary School.

A New Beginning

The Feoffees decided to make the Grammar School fee paying, some free places being available for boys from the new Elementary School. The fees for tuition were £2. per annum in 1850, £4. per annum by 1860 and £5. per annum by 1869. Up to eight boarders at £50. per annum could still be taken by the headmaster. The Rev. Lonsdale Pratt was appointed to this post in 1850 and was followed by Rev. William Hampton in 1857 and Rev. James Bennett in 1860.

James Bennett was 31 years of age when he came to Solihull with his young wife, Mary. The following year, when the census was taken, there was only one boarder, Stephen Bennett aged 14 years, perhaps a relation. Rev. Bennett was very concerned about the well-being of his pupils and condition of the school buildings; consequently in 1866 extensions were made. Three years later further, more expensive alterations and repairs were carried out, and gas lighting was installed. The enlarging and improving of the buildings made it easier to accommodate Mr. Bennett's own increasing family, for by 1871 he had eight children and there were three servants in the house. In 1876 he asked for an increase in salary and pointed out the inadequacies of the schoolhouse with regard to taking boarders. An architect inspected the building and considered part of it to be unsafe, but the Feoffees did not agree.

In 1879 the school ceased to be controlled by the Feoffees and a Board of Governors took over the management. Under a new scheme for administering the charity lands the Solihull Charity Estate was created, the revenue of its properties being mostly devoted to educational purposes. At the first meeting of the Governors James Bennett announced his resignation. He had done a great deal for the school; under his leadership the syllabus was widened, and a foundation of sound work laid which set the school on the way to greater improvement.

The Governors realised that to progress further a new building was needed. A site was acquired in Warwick Road and building began. Under the new headmaster. Rev. Robert Wilson, work continued at Park Road; there were 45 pupils, 16 being boarders, their ages ranging from six to 20 years. The census of 1881 shows that some boys were fairly local, from Edgbaston, Sutton Coldfield and Coventry, but others came from Finsbury, Cumberland, Guernsey and one from Cape Colony. Somehow Rev. Wilson managed to accommodate 24 people, including servants and his family, in the schoolhouse.

In June 1882 the new school was opened. By 1890 there were 100 pupils, and the school continued to grow in both numbers and reputation. Science and arts departments were added and a large area of the surrounding land was acquired for playing fields — a long sighted investment by the then headmaster. In 1913 the school dropped the 'Grammar' from its name and became Solihull School.

Rear view of Malvern House in 1976, when it was almost a ruin and occupied by vagrants,
showing some of the 16th century timbering and many later additions.

Malvern House. Rear view 1976, the wing, right, is a 19th century extension.

The Priory, Church Hill, demolished 1889. Here John Powell, once the usher at the Grammar School, had a most successful private school.

Glossary

ANDIRON — a firedog consisting of a pair of vertical standards each with a horizontal billet bar riveted to it. Used for supporting the logs of a wood fire.

BAND — a collar; often ornamental and in the 17th century stiffened, hence 'framework' or 'standing' band.

BAY — a structural division of a building defined by the principal supporting members, usually the main trusses of a roof.

BOLT, BOULT (to) — to sift.

BOULTING HOUSE — where meal, flour, etc., was sifted.

BONE LACE — an early name for bobbin lace; usually of linen thread and made by knitting upon a pattern marked by pins with bobbins made of bone.

BROCHE — a spit on which meat, birds etc., were roasted.

BUCK (to) — to wash, boil, bleach or dress.

BUTTERY — store room originally for drink. Later used as a cool room for food, provisions, table ware and cooking utensils.

BUTTS — a mound in front of which the targets were placed for archery practice. This was supposed to take place every Sunday morning. It was the Constable's duty to provide and maintain the parish butts.

CALASH — a light carriage with low wheels, having a removable folding hood.

CAMBRIC — a kind of fine white linen, originally made at Cambray in Flanders.

CAUL, CALL, CALLIS - a woman's round cap of net worn at the back of the head. It might be of gold thread trimmed with lace, jewels etc.

CHAFF — cut hay and straw used for feeding cattle and to fill the mattresses of poorer people.

CHANTRY — an endowment for the maintenance of an altar or chapel and a priest to sing masses, usually for the soul of the founder and his family.

CHARGER — a large plate or dish.

COBBARD, COBIRON — bars fitted with hooks which lean back from the hearth into the chimney and support broches (spits).

COFFER — a small chest, often used to store valuables, perhaps with a canted lid.

COIF, QUIFE — a close fitting cap covering the head. Usually white, often edged with lace.

CLOSE STUDDING — a type of timber framing where the main frame of each storey is divided into narrow panels by vertical timbers.

COOLER — also known as a Led. A vat for cooling ale, during brewing. Often placed in a Curb — a shallow tray to catch any overflow.

CROSS-CLOTH — a linen cloth worn across the forehead.

CUTWORK - a kind of openwork embroidery or lace.

DRAWN THREAD — ornamental work done on fabrics by drawing out some of the threads to form patterns.

DRESSER — a board on which food was prepared and dressed.

DRIPPING PAN — a metal pan placed beneath meat roasting on a spit to catch the fat and juices.

ELL — a measure of length = 45 ins.

FAN — a very fashionable accessory from the 16th century, especially when of feathers.

FERRETT — narrow ribbon or tape of coarse silk or cotton used for binding.

FLAGON — a large jug to hold drink at the table; with a spout and handle.

'FLANDERES' CANDLESTICKS — probably candlesticks of Flemish design and make. These importations had large grease pans and had a great influence on English candlestick design.

FLAX AND HEMP — were prepared for use by dressing. After harvesting the bundles were dried, threshed to remove the seed, then soaked in water for 7-20 days to 'ret' or partly rot. Then the woody part of the stem was separated from the flexible fibres before combing to separate out the three qualities of fibre 1) line — made into flaxen yarn; 2) tow; 3) hurds.

FLOCK — wool refuse used for stuffing mattresses.

FURNACE — a brewing or boiling cauldron with its own heater.

GARNER — a store for grain.

GARTER — sashes of ribbon, silk, velvet, often with fringed ends, worn outside stockings to keep them up.

GAZEBO — a small garden house commanding an extensive prospect.

GIRDLE — belt for waist or hips. Often with purse, keys, fan suspended.

GRIDIRON — iron bars set in a frame and fitted with three legs and a long handle. Used to cook small pieces of meat etc., directly over the fire.

GROAT — an English coin = 4d.

HABERDASHERY — small wares — caps, hats, thread, ribbon, tape, collars, cuffs, underwear, pins, etc.

HOOD — a traditional and practical means of keeping the head and shoulders dry. Outdoor hoods were attached to capes; for indoor wear they were decorated with lace and tassels.

HOLLAND — a fine linen fabric originally from Holland.

HURDEN — strong, coarse cloth made from inferior flax and hemp.

KETTLE — open container for heating liquid; not the modern object with a spout.

KNEADING TROUGH — a wooden trough used in bread making. It had splayed sides with a partition down the middle, one side being used for dough and the other for flour.

KNITCHING — a hank or bundle of hemp or flax.

LINK BOY — a person who carried a link or torch made of tow or pitch to light people along the streets at night.

LIVERY CUPBOARD — a small cupboard in which food, drink and lighting, for use during the night, were stored.

LOOME WORK — material made on a loom.

MANTLE — a cloak or wrap.

MASK — worn as a protection for the face and very fashionable in the 17th and 18th centuries. Half masks were very popular for street wear with hoods.

MOULDING BOARD or TABLE — on which dough was kneaded and shaped before baking.

MOURNING GIFTS — gloves, hat bands, rings etc., given to friends and relatives on behalf of the deceased to wear at his funeral.

PARGET (to) — to cover with daub or plaster, often externally, the plaster being decorated with designs.

PEEL — a long handled implement of wood or iron with a flat broad blade. Used for lifting items in and out of a brick baking oven.

POINT — thread lace made wholly with a needle. Speciality of Venice.

PORRINGER — a dish from which porridge, soup or any stew-like food was eaten.

POSNET — a funnel-shaped saucepan with a long handle and three legs.

POTHOOKS and HANGLES — hooks and hangles for hanging cooking pots and pans above the fire. Often secured into the chimney wall or from an iron bar.

QUERN — a handmill.

SAUCER — a sauce boat, not a saucer to a cup.

SCOTCH CLOTH — fabric resembling lawn but cheaper, said to have been made in the 17th century out of nettle fibre.

SCREEN FAN — a fan to protect the face from the fire.

SETTLE — a bench type seat, always with arms. Often used as a bed.

SKIMMER — a round, dished ladle with holes, used for taking the cream from milk.

SLEEVES — possibly some sort of stiff lining to help sleeves keep their shape. Alternatively, perhaps deep falling cuffs of lace or pleated lawn.

STOOLE WORK — embroidery made upon a stool or frame.

TAFFETY, TASFITY — taffeta. A silk-like material with a lustrous finish.

TALLOW — fat, especially that of sheep or oxen, used in candle making.

TESTER — a canopy over a bed, made of wood or material.

TIMBER FRAMED (building) — one in which interlocking vertical and horizontal timbers form the structural framework. The interstices being filled with non-structural walling of wattle and daub, brickwork, etc.

TOD (of wool) — two stone = 28 lbs. 60 tod of wool = 1 wey.

TWIG, TWIGGEN — wicker or rush work.

VENICE GLASS — glass made in Venice and imported into England. Only found in the houses of the better-off.

YEELING, YELING (vat, house) — a vessel or place where wort was put to ferment during the brewing process.

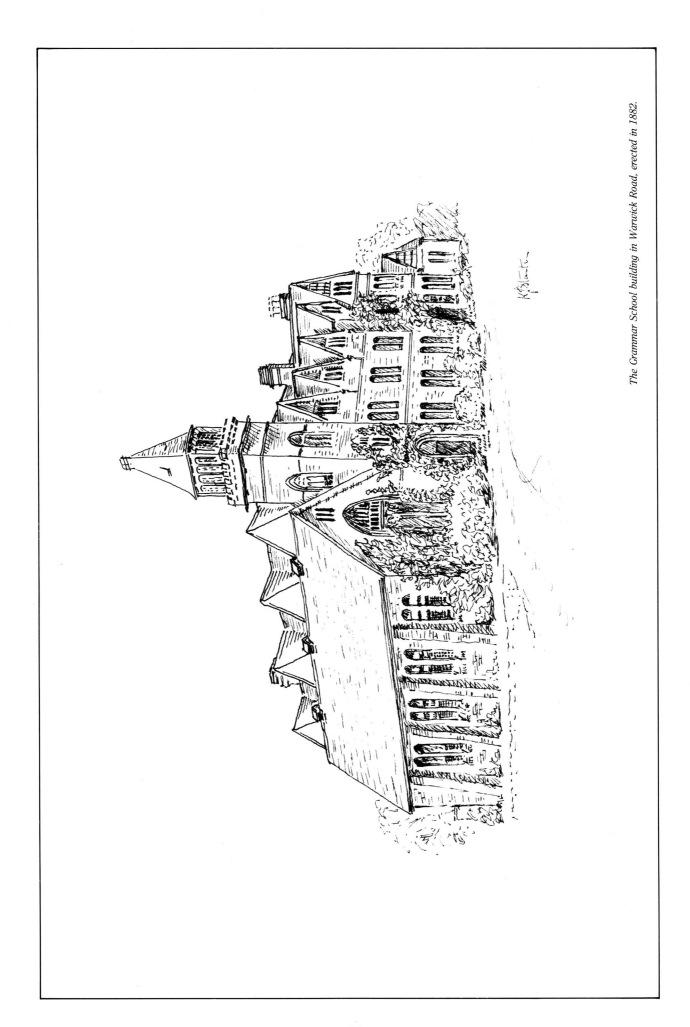

The Grammar School building in Warwick Road, erected in 1882.

66

Sources and Bibliography

Tithe Apportionment for Solihull c.1840 at Warwick County Record Office.

Anon, *Sketch of Solihull* (1840).

Census Returns for Solihull, 1841; 1861; 1871; 1881; at W.C.R.O.

Directories.

Ordnance Survey, *Warwickshire 1st. Edn. 6" 1886; 25" 1887.*

Geoffrey A. Martineau, Reminiscences of Solihull 1863 —

Solihull Parish Magazine, June 1933 — September 1934.

Solihull Parish Magazine, 1879 — 1884.

Birmingham University Extra-Mural Group 1960 — 1974; Unpublished papers.

Birmingham Daily Mail, 19th November 1903.

Birmingham Post, 12th March 1954.

Victor Skipp, *Origins of Solihull* (1977).

Chris. J. Smith, *Civic Heraldry in Warwickshire* (1973).

Reminiscences of various persons.

J. Woodall & M. Varley, *Solihull Place Names* (1979).

Solihull Court Rolls at British Museum.

Survey of Solihull Manor 1606; 1629; 1632; at Bodleian Library, Oxford.

Solihull Parish Book 1525-1720, Transcribed by G. L. Bishop (1977).

Solihull Parish Registers 1538—1668 (1904).

Wills and Inventories at Lichfield Joint Record Office.

Solihull Deeds at W.C.R.O.

R. Pemberton, *Solihull and Its Church* (1905).

Victoria County History of Warwickshire, Vol. 4.

National Dictionary of Biography.

Historical Account of the Life and Parentage of Beau Feilding Cornhill, London (1707).

Quarter Sessions Records 1682—1690, Warwick County Records Vol. 8.

J. Hannett, *Forest of Arden* (1863).

Ordnance Survey, *Geological Drift Map SP 17* 1980.

A. H. Smith, *Place-Name Elements*, English Place-Names Society Vols. 25, 26 (1970).

Archer Deeds for Solihull and Tanworth-in-Arden at Shakespeare Birthplace Record Office.

Field walking by E. M. Varley and others.

Archer Survey of 1500 at S.B.R.O.

Solihull Archaeological Group, News Sheet (1971).

S. J. Price, Interim Report on the History and Architecture of Shelly Farm, Typescript in Historical Buildings File, Local History Dept., City Museum and Art Gallery, Birmingham. (1987).

Solihull Tithe 1789 at Birmingham Reference Library.

Solihull Rate Book 1806 at Solihull Central Library.

John Burman, *Solihull and Its School* (1949).

W. Field, *Memoirs of the Life and Writings and Opinions of Samuel Parr* (1828).

Cottages in Park Road, now the site of the Crown Office.

Ivy Cottages which stood in Hampton Lane between Warwick Road and School Road and backed on to Solihull School playing fields.

Index

Bethel Chapel